rethink
severe mental illness

JENNIFER RANKIN

ippr

The **Institute for Public Policy Research** (ippr) is the UK's leading progressive think tank and was established in 1988. Its role is to bridge the political divide between the social democratic and liberal traditions, the intellectual divide between academia and the policy making establishment and the cultural divide between government and civil society. It is first and foremost a research institute, aiming to provide innovative and credible policy solutions. Its work, the questions its research poses and the methods it uses are driven by the belief that the journey to a good society is one that places social justice, democratic participation and economic and environmental sustainability at its core.

For further information you can contact ippr's external affairs department on info@ippr.org, you can view our website at www.ippr.org and you can buy our books from Central Books on 0845 458 9910 or email ippr@centralbooks.com.

Our trustees

CONTENTS

About the author

Jennifer Rankin is a researcher in health and social care policy at the ippr. Her publications include *Meeting Complex Needs: The Future of Social Care* and *Who Cares? Building the Social Care Workforce*. She has also written for the December 2004 issue of ippr's journal *New Economy*.

About Mental Health in the Mainstream

This work has been made possible through the generous support of Rethink severe mental illness, through its Mental Health First programme. The Mental Health First programme is supported by Lilly and donations from members of Rethink and its supporters.

Acknowledgements

Throughout the Mental Health in the Mainstream project, ippr has had input from an external steering group. We would like to thank all the members of this group for their ongoing involvement in the project and the time spent reading and commenting on the drafts of the working papers and final report: Janey Antoniou, Prof. Martin Knapp (LSE), Deborah Roche (formerly ippr, now at the DH). And at Rethink: Paul Corry, Paul Farmer, Alison Faulkner, Vanessa Pinfold, Dennis Preece, Cliff Prior and Kerry Williams.

The author is extremely grateful to everyone who commented on a draft of this report. In particular I would like to thank Dr Jed Boardman and Michael Parsonage at the Sainsbury Centre for Mental Health for their helpful comments. I am grateful to my ippr colleagues for their valuable input and advice: Jessica Allen, Peter Robinson and Kate Stanley. Thanks to John Schwartz and Nick Thorner at ippr for the formatting of the papers and final report. All errors and omissions are the author's responsibility alone.

The project as a whole has benefited from very useful discussions with a number of people. I would like to thank: Victor (Lord) Adebowale at Turning Point; Professor Peter Beresford at Brunel University; Angela Greatley at the Sainsbury Centre for Mental Health; Dr Matthew Broome at the Institute of Psychiatry; Gary Butcher at Rethink; Sophie Corlett at Mind; Dr Chris Fitch at the Royal College of Psychiatrists' Research Unit; Carole Furnivall at The First Step Trust; Rowan Livingstone at Social Link; Dr David Morris at the National Institute for Mental Health in England; Julia (Baroness) Neuberger; Dr Rachel Perkins at South West London and St George's Mental Health NHS Trust and Liz Sayce at the Disability Rights Commission. I am also grateful to all the participants involved in the two policy seminars held over 2004/5.

Finally, I am very grateful to all the service users, carers and service managers at Rethink for giving up their time to make the qualitative research possible. Sincere thanks go to users and carers for sharing their experiences with researchers at ippr and Rethink.

Foreword
Nick Pearce, ippr and Cliff Prior, Rethink

Poor mental health is one of the biggest social problems facing the UK. It is linked to family breakdown, poverty and worklessness. Individually and collectively, we pay a high price for mental health problems. For people with severe mental illness the price is reduced life expectancy, discrimination and social exclusion. This report's focus on making mental health a 'mainstream issue' that commands universal support is critical.

Mental health has been one of the three top priorities for the health service and there have been some substantial improvements in services. Yet in many respects there remains a clear gap between the policy vision and its implementation. Many people feel frustrated and let down. This is especially true in relation to access to psychological therapies. Now that the NHS as a whole is showing signs of sustained improvement, it is time to be more ambitious about the goals of the health system in promoting complete health, including mental health. Nine out of ten mental health problems are seen in primary care and many people with long term mental health problems are only seen in primary care. However many GPs lack the time and the resources to support people. This report sets out a new vision of community based primary care, which promotes both mental and physical health together.

But mental health is much more than the business of the health service. *Mental health in the mainstream* makes the argument that mental health should be universally valued. For too long mental health has been neglected and stigmatised or overlooked by policymakers without a specialist interest. Delivering a mentally healthy society requires a step change in levels of leadership and commitment from central and local government, employers, schools, the voluntary sector. If people make this change, the rewards are great indeed.

Executive summary

Poor mental health is one of the biggest social issues in the UK today. At any one time, one in six people experience mental health problems, which can have high costs for the individuals and their families. Beyond this, poor mental health has a significant impact on national prosperity and well-being. It is inextricably linked to the causes and consequences of many major public policy issues, including poverty and exclusion, worklessness, crime, chronic illness, low educational attainment, anti-social behaviour and lack of social cohesion.

This report sets out why mental health should be a mainstream political priority for policy-makers. It puts forward a vision of what our response to mental health could look like in 2025. Specifically, this report focuses on how the health system can be improved to offer better support for people with mental health problems and promote the mental health of the whole community.

What is mental health?

Too often, mental health is conflated with mental health problems. But mental health should be considered as a positive resource that needs to be nurtured. Central government, local government, local communities and public services all play a role in contributing to mental health. There is increasing interest in what governments should do to promote mental health and happiness.

The scope of mental health problems

The variation in mental health problems represents a challenge for policy-makers. On one side there are problems with a comparatively low incidence but high cost, such as schizophrenia and manic depression. On the other side, there are problems with a high incidence but lower cost, such as depression, stress and anxiety. Policy-makers need to design a system that meets the needs of people who fall into either category; arguably something that has not always been done successfully.

While mental health problems can affect anyone, some groups have an elevated risk of developing problems, or of being diagnosed with a mental illness. These include people living in poverty, people from some black and minority ethnic communities, people with chronic illness and people in the criminal justice system.

Mental health problems account for an increasing share of the proportion of ill-health. For example, in the 1990s the largest group of people claiming Incapacity Benefit had back pain; in 2005 the largest group of claimants had depression (Henderson et al 2005). According to the World Health Organisation, by 2020 depression will be the leading cause of disability and the second biggest contributor to illness after coronary heart disease in the developed world (WHO 2001).

It was estimated in 2002 that around one third of GPs' time is taken up by mental health problems (Sainsbury Centre 2002). However, although poor mental health has a substantial impact on the NHS, most mental health problems go untreated. In 2000, less than a quarter of people assessed were receiving treatment of any kind (Singleton et al 2000).

Poor mental health denies people many opportunities. In the UK in 2004 there were more than 900,000 people claiming Incapacity Benefit due to mental health problems (DWP 2004). This represented more than the total number who were receiving JobSeeker's Allowance. People with long-term mental health problems also have a lower life expectancy and are more likely to have problems with their physical health.

Mental health problems have a wider impact beyond those individuals who experience them first-hand. In 2000, as many as 1.5 million people were caring for relatives with mental health problems (Arksey 2002). Carers of people with long-term health problems also have a greater risk of experiencing mental health problems themselves.

The UK also pays a high price in economic terms for mental health problems. In 2003, the Sainsbury Centre for Mental Health set the annual cost of mental illness at £77.4 billion, taking into account the human costs (including mortality), the costs of health and social care, and missed employment opportunities (SEU 2004).

Public attitudes to mental health

The title of this project is Mental Health in the Mainstream. This can be understood in two senses. Firstly, it is about bringing people with mental illness into mainstream society, enabling access to opportunities for employment, leisure, and family and community life. But it is also about bringing the 'mainstream' to mental health, namely, ensuring a tolerant and realistic understanding of mental health in mainstream society, as well as a concern for good mental health. This represents a significant change in how society thinks about mental health.

The last decade has seen changing attitudes to mental health, in both positive and negative directions: there is some increased understanding of depression and stress in the workplace, but there has been a decline in tolerance for people with serious mental health problems. In recent years there have been concerted efforts to tackle the stigma of mental health problems, for example through public campaigns. Governments play a role: as the 'stewards' of mental health they need to ensure that mental health is valued and that people with mental health problems can participate in society.

Developments and trends in mental health policy

In 1997 the Government set out its top three priorities for the National Health Service: cancer, coronary heart disease and mental health. For mental health, priority status meant some new money and some new services, as well as a place in key strategies, such as the NHS Plan and the development of a National Service Framework (NSF) for Mental Health.

More broadly, Mental health services have changed substantially in the last twenty years and there have been further significant improvements since 1997. Nevertheless, for all the changes, there is a wider sense of unease that mental health has not kept pace with improvements elsewhere in the NHS. Despite the controversy over the Government's star ratings system for denoting standards, it remains significant that mental health trusts are generally below the standards of the average health trust.

Many believe that mental health services remain under-resourced, despite some additional funding since 1997. In 2002, the Wanless Report noted that spending on mental health would need to double by 2010-11, if it were to meet all the objectives as set out by the NSF (Wanless 2002). Yet it also appears that existing resources are not always used effectively, for instance there is a default reliance on medication for common mental health problems and there remain problems in inpatient care.

With regard to mental health, the health system is unbalanced. It remains overly preoccupied by a risk management agenda. Much of the energy behind recent reforms has been directed at the small group of people who are acutely unwell. This has overshadowed efforts to help others with long-term mental health problems, or people with more common experiences of depression and anxiety.

Mental health and social inclusion

By any account, people with long-term mental health problems are one of the most excluded groups in society, and social exclusion and discrimination sustain poor mental health. As such, social inclusion should be the ultimate goal of a recovery–orientated health service.

This report does not look at the many issues that relate to social inclusion, but instead concentrates on work and meaningful activity. In this area, the reforms to out-of-work disability benefits and the extension of Pathways to Work will be critical.

A vision for mental health

The development of mental health policy over the last decade shows that there are different visions about the future of mental health. This report sets out five themes to underpin a new way forward for mental health. Taken together they offer a different way of thinking about mental health.

Targeted universalism

Mental health is a universal good and there needs to be a universalist approach to meeting mental health needs and promoting mental health. However, there also needs to be particular support for people with long-term mental health problems and groups at risk of mental health problems, such as people on low incomes.

Public health

Mental health needs to be part of an ambitious strategy for public health, to foster an environment where people are encouraged to seek help early. The components of a public health approach to mental health include prevention (preventing symptoms of mental health problems and disorders) and promotion (promoting good mental health).

Social inclusion

Part of the core business of mental health services should be supporting people in living their lives and promoting opportunities and inclusion in wider society. The Government has produced strong statements of its intention to pursue the social inclusion of people with mental health problems and other disabilities (Strategy Unit 2005, SEU 2004). The implementation of the various policies will be critical, but local communities, media, private and voluntary sectors and private individuals also play a role in promoting inclusion.

Rights-based mental health

Social inclusion is most likely to succeed if it is underpinned by a rights-based approach. Important pieces of legislation include the Human Rights Act 1998 and the Disability Discrimination Acts 1995 and 2005. A rights-based approach offers practical tools to enable people to get legal redress and further social change, as well as help to create a new culture of rights.

Personalisation

At its most ambitious level, personalisation means that people are equal partners in their own treatment and care. This means developing patient-professional relationships that are non-procedural, and based on empathy and mutual respect. Involving people in their own care also means that individuals have more choice and control over treatment.

Recommendations

Following these themes, this report sets out six key recommendations for public policy.

(1) A renewed focus on primary care and community health

Community-orientated primary care should be the main driver in improving mental health services and the mental health of local communities. A new focus on community-orientated primary care would help to rebalance the health system towards more common mental health problems, as well as help to provide social support for people with long-term mental health problems.

(2) A role for access workers

This report proposes the introduction of 'access workers' as an alternative access point to GPs. Access workers would be able to offer everything from a friendly ear to professional counselling, as well as information about local support groups and sport or art on prescription. Where appropriate, they would offer people a fast and effective route into specialist services, including access to psychological treatments and medication.

Access workers may be professionals with a medical background, such as GPs with a special interest in mental health, nurses or health visitors. They may also be people from grass roots community organisations who have appropriate training. They could be based in a variety of mainstream community locations, such as Children's Centres, community centres, GPs' surgeries, libraries or Community Health Centres (see below).

(3) Development of Community Health Centres

In order to give substance to a new top-down focus on primary care, this report proposes a new grass roots organisation to develop the health and wellbeing of local communities. Community Health Centres would be walk-in centres that supported people in all aspects of a healthy life, both mental and physical.

The Centres would be designed in the community, for the community, meaning there would be no fixed blueprint for this model and it could vary according to local need. However, there would be some common principles, including the co-location of different health, social care and voluntary sector professionals. The Centres are envisaged as hubs of information and resources, supporting people to 'self-help' on all health problems.

(4) Improved access and provision of non-pharmacological treatments
If the agenda of community-based mental health is to be successful, it will require some basic changes in the provision of mental health resources. There needs to be an expansion of psychological treatments within the NHS and these should be subject to waiting lists, with corresponding targets and political pressure to reduce waiting times. There is also a need to develop knowledge about and capacity for social prescriptions, such as exercise on prescription, or books or art on prescription.

(5) Pilots of personal recovery budgets
The NHS has often proved fairly unresponsive to people's demands for different kinds of services, notably talking treatments such as seeing a psychiatrist. Introducing greater individual budget-holding, through direct payments, could help to remedy this. If people were given their own personal recovery budget they could choose their own treatment (Rankin 2005a). A personal recovery budget is, in essence, a direct payment for mental health which people can use to access services. However, if it is to work, the current direct payments system will require some adaptation.

(6) Refocusing of inpatient care
Although this report argues for a greater focus on primary care and upstream interventions, it remains vital to complete the reform of acute services. This means refocusing inpatient care so that it provides a more therapeutic environment. Research with service users and carers shows that people want some form of crisis support, a therapeutic place where people could be admitted for short periods to stabilise and manage a crisis. Refocusing inpatient care could pay dividends in improving outcomes for service users and reducing stays on inpatient wards.

Overcoming barriers to change

At times, the gap between rhetoric and reality can be especially pronounced in relation to mental health. The report looks at the key areas in which we need to overcome potential barriers to change.

Resources
It appears that mental health will need an increased share of the health budget if we are to see improvements and an expansion of provision in primary care and health promotion. As a priority, the Government should review current spending on mental health in order to answer two questions:

- Is spending cost effective? (Is it linked to services that improve outcomes?)

- Is the level of spending on particular services sufficient?

Systems and structures

In the past, major structural changes to the NHS and social care system have been the first choice for governments that have been impatient for improvement. However, there is an inherent risk that designing and redesigning systems becomes a proxy for better outcomes. For this reason, further structural change seems unhelpful. However, central government needs to ensure that the right incentives are in place for providers to supply good mental health care and for primary care trusts (PCTs) to prioritise mental health in their commissioning.

Commissioning and user involvement

The commissioning function needs to improve so that local commissioners take a strategic role in assessing need and monitoring the development of services. Mental health commissioning needs to be a collaborative enterprise, with the input of service users, local PCTs and commissioners of secondary care services. Service users should be routinely involved in setting priorities for service development.

Cultural change

The health service needs to be concerned with improving the quality of patient-professional interactions. What many people want is simply someone to talk to and a better quality of therapeutic relationships with professionals. An expansion in the provision of talking therapies needs to take place alongside a wider cultural change in health services, in which people with mental health problems are treated with kindness and respect.

Political ownership

Traditionally, there has been a lack of political interest in and ownership of mental health issues. The role of the Secretary of State for Health should be refocused beyond the acute care aspects of the NHS, on complete health, including mental health. But mental health touches on many areas of life beyond the health service. Local government will also play a critical leadership role in promoting the mental health of local communities.

Mental health needs to be mainstreamed across different government departments. To this end, this report proposes considering developing a role for a National Commissioner for Mental Health. The purpose of the Commissioner would not be to duplicate the position of the National Director for Mental Health (known as the 'mental health tsar') based in the health service. A National Commissioner would work with the National Director for Mental Health and would be an independent voice to champion mental health issues across different government departments.

The need to act

There are compelling reasons to act. Mental health problems have a high human cost in terms of lost opportunities, poorer health and lower life expectancy. They disproportionately affect disadvantaged groups and are bound up with poverty and social exclusion. Also, mental health problems carry substantial economic costs.

We need to provide a better response for people with mental health problems, as well as to foster a society where mental health is valued. To move towards a mentally healthy society will require sustained political leadership.

Mental health in the mainstream

This is the final report of the Mental Health in the Mainstream project. It outlines why policy-makers should prioritise mental health, and puts forward recommendations to create a better policy framework to support people with mental health problems. It argues for a move towards a preventative approach to mental health, as well as making mental health a mainstream issue across public policy. However, it does not attempt the sizeable task of setting out what all aspects of public policy would look like if all government departments and local authorities were driven by promoting mental health.

In part, the recommendations draw on the experiences and ideas of service users and carers in touch with Rethink services. This is the result of qualitative research conducted by Rethink for this report (Rethink 2005). The people who participated in the qualitative research were adults of working age, and the focus on this age group is reflected in the overall report (see appendix). This report does not examine in any detail the distinctive mental health issues related to children or older people, although many of the report's themes are of universal importance.

In addition to the qualitative research, the project is based on an extensive literature review which explored mental health trends, policy developments in health services, public health and some issues around social inclusion. The review included peer-reviewed publications, key government papers, 'grey' literature, surveys, campaign reports and research with service users.

During the research ippr interviewed a range of policy-makers. There were two policy seminars with a range of experts: one to review policy developments in mental health and another to discuss the future of mental health policy.

Although many of the themes have a universal resonance, this work is primarily focused on England with a look at some policy developments in Scotland.

Part 1 assesses the nature and scale of mental health problems and how they are understood. It outlines the incidence of mental health problems, their relationship with other social issues and their human and financial costs. It also explores public attitudes to mental health; in particular it looks at tolerance towards people with mental health problems and the public and political value placed on good mental health.

Part 2 provides an overview of recent developments and trends in mental health policy, in order to explore where the current gaps and weaknesses in policy lie. It examines the position of mental health in relation to health services more generally. Part 2 aims to shed some light on what mental health's priority status has meant in terms of resources and services, and in certain areas of policy, including public health and the personalisation agenda. This part also considers the social exclusion of people with mental health problems and the social marginalisation of carers. However, this is not an exhaustive survey of policy developments and does not examine every area that is relevant to mental health.

From this basis, Part 3 looks to the future of mental health. It sets out five guiding themes for mental health: targeted universalism, public health, social inclusion, rights-based mental health and personalisation. It argues that these themes should underpin the reform of services and a new political conception of mental health. Finally, it puts forward a series of six key policy recommendations and some suggestions for overcoming potential barriers to change, so that mental health really can become a mainstream issue.[1]

---

1 This report draws on the working papers of the *Mental Health in the Mainstream* series (www.ippr.org). In particular, chapter 3 reprises some of the material of working paper one, chapter 4 relates to working paper two and chapter 6 revisits the theme of choice that was addressed in the third working paper.

Introduction
Mental health in 2025

It is 2025 and a new government has recently been voted into office. As usual, health was at the top of the electorate's priorities and the election was dominated by claims and counter-claims about which party could best improve the health and wellbeing of the nation. Some of the older commentators remember the days when politicians only talked about fixing the NHS.

One of the biggest changes of the last twenty years is how mental health has become a central concern for policy-makers and the public alike. The way society thinks about mental health has changed. Mental health is no longer regarded as the special concern of the health service or as a subject which is only relevant to a minority. Instead it is an issue that is everybody's business. Politicians of all colours take it for granted that mental health contributes to the overall health and wellbeing of the nation.

Mental health problems have not disappeared, but admitting to them is no longer a source of social stigma. In every community there is a Community Health Centre where people can get advice on all aspects of health, including mental health. In these Centres there are access workers with whom people can discuss their health concerns. The access workers offer information about different ways to improve and maintain mental health, such as exercise, reading and volunteering. This type of walk-in, community-based support has been credited with a sharp decline in the number of prescriptions for anti-depressants.

Access workers have the appropriate training to fulfil this role. As well as being located in Community Health Centres, they are attached to GPs' surgeries and linked to schools and Children's Centres. The Community Health Centres are designed and delivered by the local community. They reflect the particular concerns of the local area, and people from all different social and ethnic backgrounds feel able to approach them.

When appropriate, the access worker can help people access specialist services. For those who need it, there is fast access to an assessment and the right kind of specialist treatment. People with mental health problems can choose between different kinds of evidence-based treatments and have control over any medication they take. Many choose psychological therapies, which are available at diagnostic and treatment centres. At the same time as receiving specialist treatment, people can access community-based support, such as help with daily life and maintaining physical health. Family and friends also use Community Health Centres, where they can access up to date information about health concerns for themselves or relatives, keep informed and help maintain their own health.

For those who need them, there are a number of dedicated crisis units, where people can access high-level support in the event of an emergency. Overall, the use of inpatient beds has fallen and the average length of stay is shorter. Crisis units are adapted from old inpatient wards. They offer people a therapeutic and homely environment when they are unwell. This means people have private rooms, access to exercise and leisure activities, and therapeutic support from staff.

For some people mental illness means they stop working or are prevented from beginning work in the first place. Where appropriate, people have a personal job broker to help them back into work and to stay in work. As a result of these initiatives, the number of people claiming out-of-work disability benefits due to mental ill-health has fallen steadily. Most employers have established policies and procedures for helping people with mental health problems in addition to the anti-discrimination policies to which they adhere.

In the public domain there is evidence of a culture shift. Individuals have good levels of knowledge of mental health and know how to protect their own. In schools, children are taught how to understand and look after their mental health. It is considered unacceptable to make derogatory remarks about mental illness. The media are sensitive to mental health issues; journalists adhere to the industry's codes and avoid using sensational language.

In 2025, mental health is universally supported and universally valued. Mental health is regarded as a positive resource and one which central and local government, employers and communities want to protect. One of the main goals of the health system is to support people in maintaining good health, including mental health. Within this universalist framework, there is a particular targeting of services and support towards people with mental health problems. An overarching concern of policy is ensuring that everyone is able to participate in society as equals.

* * *

It is a timely moment to look ahead to the future of mental health. Mental health policy is in a state of transition. At one end the debate on mental health is dominated by an old agenda of risk management and concerns over public order. At the other, there are new agendas opening up in mental health around rights and social inclusion, as well as public health and mental health promotion.

This vision of mental health in 2025 is of a health system that is focused on complete health and which is geared to maintaining and improving health. It offers a glimpse of a system in which support and information is easily accessible in community settings, where individuals and families are empowered to play a greater role in looking after their own health and where there is a clear pathway to a range of effective specialist services for those who need them. It is based on a changed cultural response to mental health: that mental health is a key political priority and an issue of public importance.

What is mental health?

Too often, mental health has been conflated with mental health problems. But mental health should be considered as a positive resource which needs to be nurtured. It has been helpfully defined as:

> The emotional and spiritual resilience that enables us to enjoy life and to survive pain, suffering and disappointment. It is a positive sense of wellbeing and an underlying belief in our own worth and the worth of others. (Health Education Authority 1997, cited in Hartley Brewer 2001).

And as:

> Essentially about how we think and feel about ourselves and about others and how we interpret the world around us. It affects our capacity to manage, to communicate and to form and sustain relationships. It also affects our capacity to cope with change and transitions such as life events – having a baby, going to prison, experiencing bereavement. Mental health may be central to all health and wellbeing because how we think and feel has a strong impact on physical health. (www.mentality.org.uk)

Central government, local government, local communities and public services all play a role in contributing to mental health. There is increasing interest in what governments should do to promote mental health and to secure happiness. Richard Layard has put forward the view that governments should aim to maximise happiness and develop public policies to reduce misery (Layard 2005a). The Nuffield Foundation has argued for the development of a 'civil society' that acknowledges responsibility for mental health and pursues co-ordinated policies (Longley et al 2001). Evidently, there is a large number of policies that affect mental health, and responsibility for mental health extends well beyond the health service.

Mental health problems

At any one time, one in six people have mental health problems. This is according to the Psychiatric Morbidity Survey conducted in 2000, which found that one in six people had common mental health problems in the week prior to interview. The same survey suggested that the prevalence rate for psychotic disorders was one per 200 (Singleton et al 2000).[2] This represents a challenge for policy-makers. On one side there are mental health problems with a comparatively low incidence but high cost, such as schizophrenia and manic depression. On the other there are problems with a high incidence but lower cost, such as depression, stress and anxiety. Policy-makers need to design a system that meets the needs of people who fall into either category; arguably something that has not always been done successfully.

There are many diagnoses, definitions and labels to describe mental health problems, and it is important to take care when discussing them. Experiences of mental ill-health are diverse. As a review conducted on behalf of the National Institute for Mental Health in England (NIMHE) has noted:

> Mental health is not a neat high ground of clear definitions and well demarcated pathways, but a messy swamp of symptoms that are often hard to disentangle and rarely conform to case definitions. (NIMHE 2002)

The same diagnosis can have very different effects on different people's lives. Likewise the same treatments are not always equally effective; not everyone fits the average. But policy-makers have often overlooked this diversity and there is a 'tendency to generalise in a world where difference is the norm'.[3] Likewise, policy-makers have also lost sight of the complexity of people's needs. Health and social care services have subdivided needs into different categories and have not been able to take a joined-up approach to people's medical, social and emotional needs (Rankin and Regan 2004). This partly reflects the historic dominance of the 'medical model', where problems have been understood through a clinical perspective. This dominance is being challenged, with greater attention given to a social model, which takes into account the social causes and consequences of health problems or disability (Salvage 2002).

This is not to suggest that practitioners should abandon diagnoses. They will remain a tool for clinicians as well as for service planners and commissioners. However, within a broader policy arena, there is a need to develop a new narrative for mental health, which takes greater account of the variation in experience of mental health problems and their effect on the wider context of people's lives. This is what this report aims to provide.

---

2 The Psychiatric Morbidity Survey collected data on the prevalence of mental health problems among adults aged 16-74 years living in private households in Great Britain. The survey covered neurosis, psychosis, alcohol misuse and drug dependence, personality disorder and self-harm.
3 I am grateful to Paul Gocke at the London Development Centre for this phrase.

Part 1

Understanding mental health

1. The scale of mental health problems

There is no health without mental health (World Federation for Mental Health).[4]

Poor mental health is one of the biggest social issues in the UK today. At any one time a large number of people experience mental health problems, which has high costs for the individuals and their families. Beyond this, poor mental health has a significant impact on national prosperity and wellbeing. Poor mental health is inextricably linked to the causes and consequences of many major public policy issues,including poverty and exclusion, worklessness, crime, chronic illness, low educational attainment, anti-social behaviour and lack of social cohesion.

The facts and figures on mental health problems are well rehearsed. They are summarised in this chapter in order to show the extent and complexity of mental health problems and their wide-ranging effects on many areas of life.

The extent of the problem

In 2000, the health system was treating around 2.5 million adults of working age for mental health problems (Singleton et al 2000). It was estimated in 2002 that around thirty per cent of all GP consultations and fifty per cent of follow-up consultations were related to mental health problems (Sainsbury Centre 2002). However, although poor mental health has a substantial impact on the NHS, most mental health problems go untreated. In 2000, less than a quarter (twenty-four per cent) of people assessed as having a neurotic disorder were receiving treatment of any kind (Singleton et al 2000).

In 2000, the World Health Organisation (WHO) estimated that mental health problems (including alcohol abuse) accounted for forty-three per cent of all years lived with a disability (WHO 2001). In the UK in 2004 there were more than 900,000 people claiming Incapacity Benefit (IB) due to mental health problems (DWP 2004). This represented more than the total number who were receiving JobSeeker's Allowance. Furthermore, once people start to claim IB their chances of working again diminish. Once someone has been claiming IB for one year, the average period of claim is eight years; after they have been claiming IB for two years, they are more likely to die or retire than to get a job (Stanley and Maxwell 2004).

---

4 www.wfmh.org

It is generally understood that mental health problems are increasing, although the extent to which this is due to an increase in the incidence of mental health problems or better diagnosis of mental ill-health is unclear. As the general UK population has become more physical healthy it appears that mental health has declined. Thus, mental health problems account for an increasing share of the proportion of ill-health. For example, in the 1990s the largest group of people claiming IB had back pain; in 2005 the largest group of claimants had depression (Henderson et al 2005). According to the WHO, by 2020 depression will be the leading cause of disability and the second biggest contributor to illness after coronary heart disease in the developed world (WHO 2001).

Poor mental health is often bound up with other complex needs, and trying to define boundaries is ultimately unhelpful. ippr has used 'complex needs' as a framework for understanding the interconnected nature of people's needs, in other words the interlocking nature of medical, social and emotional needs (Rankin and Regan 2004). People with complex needs may have mental health problems combined with substance misuse or a disability, including a learning disability. These issues are experienced alongside multiple problems of exclusion, poor housing, unemployment and few opportunities for meaningful activity or leisure. The sum of the problems may add up to more than each individual component part.

Mental health problems have a wider impact beyond those individuals who experience them first-hand. In 2000, there were seven million carers looking after sick, disabled or elderly relatives (ONS 2002). A study in 2002 estimated that as many as 1.5 million people were caring for relatives with mental health problems (Arksey 2002). The care they provide ranges from a few hours of help a week, to twenty-four-hour care. Families caring for a relative with schizophrenia provide on average six to nine hours of unpaid support every day. Those looking after relatives with dementia can be involved in caring most of the time (McDaid 2005). Caring may have an impact on the carer's own mental health, as well as on economic and social opportunities (see chapter 4). A survey in 2000-01 found that those who reported that caring affected their employment were more likely to experience mental health problems (ONS 2002). It is significant that the cost of informal care for people with mental health problems accounts for a greater proportion of costs than formal services (Knapp et al 2004).

Mental health across the life cycle

Poor mental health is a universal issue and mental health problems can affect anyone. Although this project is focused on adults of working age, it recognises that mental health is an issue at any time of life.

According to the Department of Health around ten per cent of five to fifteen year olds have a diagnosable mental health disorder; of these forty per cent are not in touch with specialist services (DH 2004a). There is some evidence to suggest that young people's mental health is getting worse. In 2004, research by the Nuffield Foundation suggested that, over the course of the last thirty years, behavioural problems have doubled and emotional problems have increased by seventy per cent (Collishaw et al 2004). It is unclear whether this is a temporary aberration or a continuing trend.

Mental health problems also have a significant impact on the lives of older people. In 2005 it was estimated there were 750,000 people with dementia and at least one million with depression. The latter figure could be an underestimate, as it is accepted that the scale of the problem is not fully understood (SEU 2005). Rates of depression are particularly high in long-term care settings (Mentality 2002).

Mental health and gender

Mental health problems vary between men and women. Women have a higher incidence of depression than men. Women are more likely to have eating disorders and to self-harm; men are more likely to have problematic use of alcohol (Singleton et al 2000). Young men are also more likely to commit suicide, although in recent years the suicide rate has been falling.[5] Women and men also experience mental health problems differently, for example men with schizophrenia are less likely to have independent living skills than women with the same diagnosis (Astbury 1999).

Who is most at risk?

While mental health problems can affect anyone, some groups have an elevated risk of developing mental health problems, or of being diagnosed with a mental illness. These include people living in poverty, people from some black and minority ethnic (BME) communities, people with chronic illness and people in the criminal justice system. There are other groups with a high risk of poor mental health who are not discussed in detail here, such as single mothers, members of the armed forces and asylum seekers.

Mental health and poverty

Poor people are more likely to suffer mental health problems. The relationship between poverty and mental health is self-sustaining. Mental health problems can make people poor and keep them poor; if people

---

5 The Government has a target on suicide reduction, which is on course to be met (DH 2004c).

become excluded from the labour market due to mental health problems, they often lose confidence, experience and skills. However, it is also true that people from poorer backgrounds are more likely to experience poor mental health in the first place. For instance, depression is around twice as prevalent among low-income groups (WHO 2001). It is believed that around ten per cent of neurotic disorder could be attributed to a low standard of living (DRC 2004). A survey by the Office of National Statistics in 1999 showed that five per cent of children from Social Class I families had mental health problems, but that they affected fourteen per cent of children from Social Class V families. In the very small number of families where neither parent has ever worked, more than twenty-one per cent of children have recognised mental health problems (Meltzer et al 2000). Being poor as a child is associated with having a long-term condition that limits work in adulthood (Sigle Ruston, 2004).

Single parents have an increased risk of depression and poor mental health, compared to the general population. In 2004, it was found that around twenty-eight per cent of all lone parents experienced common mental health problems, such as depression. This is a consequence of low employment rates and insufficient family support (SEU 2004).

People from poorer families face higher risk factors for a number of reasons, including increased risk of physical health problems, worse access to services and poor quality environments. Inequalities in mental wellbeing are connected to inequalities in physical wellbeing. The state of a neighbourhood, ranging from the condition of the built environment to people's sense of 'connectedness', that is the level of social capital, also has a significant effect on people's mental health (Mentality 2002). For instance, older people are more likely to feel lonely and isolated if they live in deprived areas (SEU 2005). The proportion of adults reporting a lack of social support increases as income levels fall (Mentality 2002).

Increasingly, it is recognised by policy-makers that it is impossible to separate physical and mental wellbeing (WHO 2001). Experiences associated with exclusion, the stress of racism, fear of crime and a sense of lack of control leave their imprint on the body, from blood pressure and cholesterol levels, to greater susceptibility to infection (Mentality 2002). There is also evidence to suggest that some people who become disabled are already disadvantaged, lacking a job and skills before developing an impairment (Stanley and Regan 2003).

People from poorer backgrounds are less likely to benefit from the public services designed to reduce or alleviate health problems. There is an inverse care law for people with complex needs, in that people most in need of support often receive the least effective intervention (Rankin and Regan 2004). Due to the complexity of the issues, people have tended to get a fragmented response from services; for example some services address substance misuse without looking at mental health issues, or offer support for mental health problems but none for getting a job. Health inequalities are partly related to access to services. People from higher socio-economic groups are more likely to benefit from interventions that are preventative or therapeutic (Acheson 1998). Also, people from poorer backgrounds are more likely to feel that their health is beyond their control (Heer and Woodhead 2004).

Mental health and ethnicity

Mental health problems vary across different BME communities, although it is generally true that people from ethnic minorities have a worse experience of mental health services than others. People from ethnic minority backgrounds are less likely than other people to visit GPs for stress or emotional problems (O'Connor and Nazroo 2002). In 2005, rates of suicide and self-harm were sixty per cent higher for young Asian girls than the average for their white counterparts (DH 2005a)

African-Caribbean men have a significantly higher chance of being diagnosed with schizophrenia and receiving coercive treatments, such as treatment under compulsory section (Keating et al 2002). A study in 2000 suggested that rates of schizophrenia were also higher among second generation African-Caribbeans, in comparison to the first generation who originally migrated to the UK. Various social reasons have been suggested to explain this fact, including institutional and individual racism, low employment levels, poor housing and a lack of cultural identity (Bhugra 2000). African-Caribbean men are less likely than whites to be diagnosed with depression or offered some kind of therapeutic intervention, such as counselling (Keating et al 2002).

According to the National Director for Mental Health, 'the needs of black and minority ethnic communities is the area where there is the greatest need and yet the least has been done' (Forrest 2005). In 2005 the Government published an action plan for tackling discrimination for all BME patients. Among the priorities, the plan aims to reduce fear of mental health services, offer more balanced therapies and increase user satisfaction (DH 2005b).

Mental health and caring

Carers of people with long-term illnesses or mental illnesses are more likely than non-carers to experience distress and depression. There is a direct relationship between care giving and distress, which is independent of physical health problems, financial strains, employment status and social background (SPRU 2004). Awareness of carers' mental health problems has spurred greater efforts to support carers through carers' support plans and provision of respite care (DH 2002, DH 1999). But despite growing attention in health and social services, carers' needs often go unnoticed in society at large (see chapter 4).

Mental health and chronic illness

People with long-term health problems have a higher risk of common mental health problems. This is true of people with chronic physical illnesses, as well as long-term severe mental illness. Evidence from the WHO shows that people with stroke or cancer have a three times higher risk of major depression than the risk facing the general population. Moreover they are less likely to adhere to medical treatment and have a higher risk of disability and premature death (WHO 2003).

Mental health and the prison population

The prevalence of mental health problems in prisons differs substantially from the general population. In a survey conducted by the ONS in 1997, nine in ten prisoners showed signs of having a mental health problem.[6] Many prisoners have more than one diagnosis, with rates for multiple problems especially high for prisoners on remand as opposed to sentenced prisoners (Singleton et al 1998). The Government recognises the high level of mental health problems in prisons. In 2004 the Minister for Community Care told the Parliamentary Joint Committee on Human Rights, 'a horrifying level of people … have a mental health disorder in prison' (House of Commons/House of Lords 2004). The continuation of mental health problems on release is just one of many factors that contribute to significant levels of recidivism. This is especially true for short-stay prisoners who complete most of their sentence on remand. The majority of people held on remand (usually young men) are in prison for a relatively short period, but there is relatively limited help to assist them in turning their lives around (Howard League for Penal Reform 2003).

Why do mental health problems matter?

However, statistics alone do not adequately convey the impact of mental health problems on individual lives, or on the national economy and well-being. Although not exactly unique, mental health problems have an unusually broad impact on all aspects of life.

---

6 The survey looked for personality disorder, psychosis, neurosis, alcohol misuse and drug disorder.

Mental health is probably the single biggest cause of misery in the country. The National Child Development Survey provides evidence that poor mental health accounts for more unhappy people than low income does, even after allowing for the effect of low income on mental health (Layard 2005b).

People with serious mental health problems also have poorer health and life expectancy. Studies in the US have shown that a person with a severe mental illness dies nine years earlier than average (DRC 2004). In their lifetime, they are more likely to experience chronic health problems, such as diabetes and cardiovascular disease, but less likely to be the recipients of health promotion activities, such as smoking cessation programmes, blood pressure checks or prescriptions for exercise (DRC 2004).

People who experience serious mental health problems are disadvantaged in many areas of life. In 2004 only about a quarter of people with long-term mental health problems worked, even though many more wanted to. This is the lowest rate of employment among all groups of disabled people. People who act as carers for people with long-term health problems have a different, but related experience of disadvantage in the labour market. They are more likely to work fewer hours, and receive lower wages in work and lower pensions on retirement (Seddon et al 2004, Evandrou and Glaser 2003).

Mental ill-health carries high human costs in terms of lost years, missed opportunities and poor health. But as well as the human justifications for responding to mental health problems, any government should be concerned with the financial impact of poor mental health. In 2003, the Sainsbury Centre for Mental Health set the annual cost of mental illness at £77.4 billion, taking into account the human costs (including mortality), costs of health and social care, and missed employment opportunities (SEU 2004). In 2002/3, around thirteen per cent of the hospital and community health service budget was spent on mental health services, although most of this was directed towards a small number of people (Rankin 2004). In developed countries, between thirty-five and forty-five per cent of absenteeism at work is due to mental health problems (WHO 2003).

The 'hidden' costs of mental illness have a significant impact on the public finances: it has been estimated that the costs of depression on employment are twenty-three times greater than the costs to the health service (Knapp 2003). By age twenty-eight, a person who had a childhood conduct disorder has cost society ten times more than an average person (Knapp et al 2004).

From whichever perspective, it is clear that the UK pays a high price for mental health problems. The shadow of mental ill-health falls heavily on people's lives and extracts a heavy cost from the public finances and national prosperity. As such mental health should be an issue of major concern for the government and for the public. But as the next chapter will discuss, this is not always the case.

2. Attitudes to mental health

Governments...are the ultimate stewards of mental health. (WHO 2001)

The title of this project is *Mental Health in the Mainstream*. This can be understood in two senses. First, it is about bringing people with mental illness into mainstream society, enabling access to opportunities for employment, leisure, and family and community life. But it is also about bringing 'the mainstream' to mental health, namely, ensuring a tolerant and realistic understanding of mental health in mainstream society, as well as a concern for good mental health. This represents a significant change in how society thinks about mental health.

There are two interrelated issues: first, the prioritisation of mental health; second, promoting tolerance and understanding towards people with mental health problems. On both issues there are reasons to be pessimistic. Mental health is not a priority in the public debate on health, whilst discussion on mental health problems is mostly focused at the extremes. The media do not consistently adhere to the Press Complaints Commission code, which states that reporting on mental health should avoid prejudice or pejorative reference. According to a government report, whereas the issues of race and sexuality have benefited from anti-stigma and anti-discrimination campaigns, mental health has seen the least progress (SEU 2004). Some commentators have observed the way society treats people with severe mental illness and have taken it as an indicator of a wider moral decline (Neuberger 2005).

However, there is more understanding of common mental health problems. Over the last two decades there has been some increase in tolerance and understanding of stress in the workplace and depression (Smith 2002). But this has not given way to a positive understanding of mental health as a state of wellbeing, autonomy and resilience. It remains true that mental health is mostly conflated with mental health problems. The issue of good mental health has been much less visible in the national debate on public health than issues surrounding physical health, such as obesity and smoking.

This chapter considers the public debate on mental health. It looks at how some policy-makers have begun to change the terms of the debate, which could offer reasons for optimism in the future.

The prioritisation of mental health

When politicians want to praise or (more typically) criticise the Government's management of the NHS they sometimes take up the case of an individual patient. In the 1992 election campaign the Labour party used the case of 'Jennifer's ear'; in 2005 the Conservatives used the case of 'Margaret's shoulder'. It is hard to think of a politician of any party taking up the case of 'somebody's mind' to make points about the way the Government of the day oversees the NHS. This is partly because politicians respond to what they believe to be the electorate's priorities.

Despite the prevalence of mental health problems and their damaging social and economic effects, mental health does not feature highly among people's priorities for the health service. In a poll conducted by MORI in 2003 that asked people which illnesses or diseases should be national priorities, fewer people mentioned mental health than other major health problems. This remains true even when various forms of mental health problem are added together. Over a quarter (seventy-six per cent) of respondents mentioned cancer as a priority, forty-seven per cent coronary heart disease, fifteen per cent Alzheimer's, thirteen per cent mental illness, seven per cent depression and four per cent anxiety (MORI 2003). Of course, political priorities are not a zero sum gain – we do not need to care less about cancer to care more about mental health – but what is interesting is how some illnesses have become more important priorities over the last few decades. For example the WHO observes that cancer has changed from being a 'family secret' that wasn't openly discussed, to a cause of national importance (WHO 2001).

While people may not prioritise mental health, there is greater understanding of particular conditions like depression. In the last twenty years books about depression have become more commonplace and attitudes have become less stigmatising (Smith 2002). The issue of stress in the workplace is widely accepted. But despite these facts, personal experiences of physical health problems remain much better understood than experiences of mental ill-health. Part of the reason may be that mental health problems are mostly invisible. This fact was picked up in focus groups with people who use mental health services and their carers.

> Some sorts of illnesses like depression, members of the public, they can't identify, they don't take notice that you've got depression ... I mean you can't notice that ... So they can't do anything ... I mean with a leg injury you can notice or something physical. But with mental illness, how can you know? (Rethink 2005).

Despite the existence of user/survivor movements, there is no widespread campaign for better mental health services, as there was for 'shorter waiting lists' in 1997 or 'better school meals' in 2005. As Richard Layard has observed, most people with mental health problems lead lives of 'quiet, grey desperation'. They do not agitate for better services (Layard 2005b).

The language of mental health also mitigates against clear understanding. The phrase 'mental health' can be unclear or confusing. When most people hear 'mental health', they understand it as 'mental health problems'. When asked to list phrases to describe someone who is mentally ill, around a quarter of people did not mention any phrases to describe people, with six per cent saying they could not think of anything and eighteen per cent saying they just didn't know. The most common phrases were 'just sick/ill' and 'need help, care and attention/understanding treatment/specialist treatment', both mentioned by nine per cent of people. The next most common sets of phrases were 'depressed/manic depressive/suicidal' or 'mad/crazy/insane/mental/barmy', both at eight per cent (National Statistics 2003). However, these findings need to be offset by qualitative research conducted by the Royal College of Psychiatrists. This showed that people had a good understanding of particular problems, including severe depression, panic attacks, schizophrenia, dementia, eating disorders, alcoholism and drug addiction (Crisp et al 2000).

Over the last decade there has been an increasing recognition by academics and policy-makers of the importance of mental health as part of complete health and wellbeing. The WHO has published several key reports that make the case for why national governments should take mental health more seriously (WHO 2001, WHO 2003). But in England this message has little resonance amongst the wider public. The national debate on public health is mostly centred on protecting physical health, rather than mental health. This may be because the incidence of mental health problems is less well understood than physical problems. There is a tendency to underestimate the commonness of mental health problems. When asked in 2003 to comment on how common mental health problems were, a quarter of people thought they affected one in ten people, while thirty-eight per cent thought they affected fewer people than this (National Statistics 2003).

Public tolerance

If people generally underestimate the prevalence of common mental health problems, they overestimate the risks associated with severe mental health problems. In recent years tolerance to people with mental health problems appears to have declined. According to a survey commissioned by the Department of Health, between 2000 and 2003 levels of fear and intolerance increased. People became more likely to think that it is frightening to have people with mental illnesses living in residential neighbourhoods; they were less likely to agree that less emphasis should be placed on protecting the public from people with mental illness. According to this survey, only two thirds of people think that someone with mental health problems has the same right to a job as anyone else. Nonetheless there was a contradictory recognition of the problem of stigma, with eighty-three per cent of people agreeing that society needed to take a far more tolerant attitude towards people with mental illness (National Statistics 2003).

Not all the evidence on public attitudes points in the same direction, and much depends on what survey respondents take 'mental illness' or 'mental health problems' to mean. In a survey by the Royal College of Psychiatrists, following the campaign Every Family in the Land, there was some marginal increase in tolerance, with five per cent fewer people believing that schizophrenia was dangerous. The public response to a very negative, stigmatising front page by the Sun newspaper is also interesting. On 23 September 2003, the Sun published two very different headlines about the story of the boxer Frank Bruno, who was being treated as an inpatient. 'Bonkers Bruno Locked Up' was changed to 'Sad Bruno in Mental Home' for later editions, after an outcry from the paper's readers. It is difficult to be sure whether this reveals people's attitudes to mental health, or to a popular sports personality.

When celebrities are not involved, media interest is often focused on the extremes and preoccupied with risk. In the mid-1990s one study concluded that two thirds of all media reports in the UK portrayed people with mental health problems as violent, while forty per cent of daily tabloid articles and forty-five per cent of Sundays used language such as 'nutter' and 'loony' (Mental Health Foundation 2000). As Liz Sayce at the Disability Rights Commission has written, 'there still appears to be no taboo against viewing psychiatric patients as "guilty until proven innocent"' (Sayce 2004). The number of murders committed by people with serious mental health problems is around forty a year, a figure that has remained stable for the last fifty years, whilst other murders have risen (SEU 2004). To put this into perspective: for every person who is the victim of a murder committed by someone with a known mental illness, seventy people will be killed in car accidents (SEU 2004).

> Most of us do not think that we will be killed by an aeroplane crash, struck by lightning, poisoned by a badly fitted gas appliance or drown when swimming for pleasure, even though all these activities have a higher risk than that of being killed by a stranger with mental illness. (www.rcpsych.ac.uk)

Of course, no statistical comparison can be of any consolation when these rare murders occur. Clearly, there does need to be a policy response on managing risk, but this needs to be proportionate to the risk presented. Most people would find it odd if the Government's policy on fathers was determined by managing the risk posed by the very small number of fathers who were also abusive towards their partners. It is also important to look at risk from the perspective of people with severe mental illnesses, who are more likely to be the victims of crime. One study of people with a diagnosis of psychosis showed that they were less likely to be arrested for violent crimes than the general population, and fourteen times more likely to be the victim of a violent crime than to be arrested for one (Ryan 2002).

Despite this, over the last decade risk management has taken a more central place in mental health policy. Since the early 1990s mental health service users have been increasingly defined in terms of risk to others, which raises the danger of people being excluded from decisions about their lives. In one study of mental health service users, the majority were not aware that professionals were formally assessing risks. Few professionals made these assessments through formal, systematic evaluations and there were some examples of inaccurate or vague information about risk (Langan and Lindow 2004). Observers have noted an increasingly custodial atmosphere in mental health hospitals (Laurance 2003). In the decade between 1988 and 1998, total detentions under the Mental Health Act rose every year, from 24,811 in 1987/8 to 46,003 in 1998/9.[7] There has also been an increase in the number of people detained under the Mental Health Act and in the number of secure beds, especially in London (McCrone et al 2003, DH 2005a). There is a need for a more precise understanding as to why the closure of old psychiatric hospitals has been followed by a substantial growth of care in more restrictive care settings. More careful scrutiny of the coercive aspects of the mental health system is essential to ensure that overall goals of rights and inclusion are not displaced by risk management and exaggerated public fears.

In England, the last few years have been dominated by a bitter debate over the proposals of the Government's Mental Health Bill, which proposes to extend compulsory treatment, even when therapeutic value cannot be proven. In 2005 the Government's proposals were criticised by the Joint Committee on the Draft Mental Health Bill for placing too much emphasis on protecting the public from a very small number of dangerous mentally ill people. The Joint Committee recommended tightening the criteria for compulsory treatment so that it applies to people who pose 'a significant risk of harm to others' rather than for 'the protection of other persons' (Joint Committee 2005). Mental health policy and legislation should not be driven by a preoccupation with the risk of violence.

A new approach to mental health

There have been more positive messages about tackling mental health problems. In 2004 the Social Exclusion Unit (SEU) published a major

---

7 This rise has now stabilised and fallen in recent years. In 2003–04 the number of detentions under the Mental Health Act was 43,847. Figures from the Department of Health.

report examining the pernicious and enduring links between poor mental health and social exclusion. This included an action plan with strategies on employment, health and social care services and communities, which will be carried out under the leadership of the National Institute for Mental Health in England (NIMHE) (SEU 2004). There have also been campaigns aimed at raising awareness and reducing stigma of mental health issues, such as the Department of Health campaign Mind Out for Mental Health and the Royal College of Psychiatrists campaign Every Family in the Land. The National Service Framework for Mental Health and the Government's Public Health White Paper both emphasise the importance of mental health in the context of public health (DH 2004b, DH 1999).

It could be argued that some inconsistency in the message from central government is inevitable, given the diversity of mental health problems. Yet lessons from other countries suggest inconsistency does not need to be inherent. It is possible to set a clear, consistent, positive message on mental health. The New Zealand government ran the campaign Like Minds to change attitudes to mental health. Among the general population there was an increase in awareness of common mental health problems and people with mental health problems reported an increase in acceptance. However, the initial stages of the campaign have been less focused on serious mental health problems such as schizophrenia, and as such there was much less impact on the perception of these (Akroyd and Wyllie 2002).

In Scotland, a high-profile campaign See Me was launched in 2002. This is funded by the Scottish Executive, and promoted and managed by grass-roots organisations.[8] The level of funding is comparatively high: the campaign spends around thirteen pence per head of the population, compared with 1.44 pence spent per capita by Mind Out for Mental Health and forty-four pence spent by Like Minds (SEU 2004). The campaign uses a variety of media, including TV and radio. Although it is too soon to reach a judgement on its long-term effects, research by the Scottish Executive suggests it has had some initial impact. The proportion of people who associated mental health with dangerousness fell by seventeen percentage points in two years, whilst there were smaller falls (of five percentage points) in the number who said they wouldn't want anyone knowing if they had mental health problems (Braunholtz et al 2004).

In 2004 the Department of Health launched a new campaign to tackle stigma and discrimination in England against people with mental health problems: Shift. It has drawn on many of the lessons of successful campaigns. A scoping review, published by NIMHE (2004) made the following recommendations:

---

8 The Scottish Executive has inaugurated a National Programme for Mental Health and Wellbeing – see chapter 3 for discussion (Scottish Executive 2004).

- Users and carers are involved throughout the design, delivery, monitoring and evaluation of anti-discrimination programmes.

- National programmes should support local activity and demonstrate the most potent combination for efficacy.

- Programmes should address behaviour change with a range of approaches.

- Clear, consistent messages are delivered in targeted ways to specific audiences.

- Long-term planning and funding underpins programme sustainability.

- Programmes should be appropriately monitored and evaluated.

The target groups for the NIMHE campaign are young people, public sector organisations, private, voluntary and professional organisations, the media and the public. It is too early to measure the impact of this campaign; however, as with any campaign its success will depend on many factors beyond the campaign itself, including the energy and resources devoted to mental health promotion, as well as how far central and local government pick up on the messages of the campaign.

* * *

As the WHO quotation that opened this chapter suggests, national governments have an overall responsibility to tackle mental health problems and promote the mental health of their populations. The last decades have seen changing attitudes to mental health, in both positive and negative directions. The Government needs to play a more strategic role in directing change towards understanding for people with mental health problems. It also needs to make the case for why mental health needs to be valued. This requires a long-term and sustained programme to tackle discrimination and promote mental health literacy.

Part 2

Developments and trends in mental health policy

3. Mental health and health services

All priorities are equal, but some are more equal than others.
(DH 2004)

In 1997 the Government set out its top three priorities for the National Health Service: cancer, coronary heart disease and mental health. For mental health priority status meant some new money and some new services, as well as a place in key strategies such as the NHS Plan. For the Government, the centrepiece of mental health reform was the development of a National Service Framework (NSF) for Mental Health in 1999. This outlined several key priority areas (DH 1999):

National Service Framework

- Standard 1 Mental health promotion

- Standard 2 and 3 Primary care and access to services

- Standard 4 and 5 Effective services for people with severe mental illness

- Standard 6 Carers

- Standard 7 Preventing suicide

This is more than any previous government had done to raise the profile of mental health. Mental health services have improved significantly for some people. However, in many ways the service response remains partial and inadequate. Some services lag behind far behind expectations of how they could support people. One leading clinical psychologist has argued that there are still 'ten thousand miles to go in improving mental health services' (Gillen 2005).

Despite these criticisms it is important to remember that mental health services have changed substantially in the last twenty years. In 1985, most of the resources for mental health were locked into psychiatric hospitals – the major programme of hospital closures had yet to begin and only a few community health teams existed (Boardman 2005). Service users were barely visible in relation to mental health reforms. In the discussions around the 1983 Mental Health Act service users were hardly involved, which offers a marked contrast to the discussions around the reform of the

Mental Health Bill, where service users have been prominent (Campbell 2005).

It is important not to forget these transformations. But nevertheless, for all the changes, there is a wider sense of unease that mental health has not kept pace with improvements elsewhere in the NHS. Mental health appears to trail behind new developments in the health service, from new policies on choice to falling behind in the National Programme for IT (Forrest 2004, Forrest 2005). This may indicate uncertainty about where mental health belongs in the health service: is it a small part of health services, or does mental health belong in the mainstream of health policy?

Evidence on the satisfaction of people who use mental health services is varied. In 2004, a survey of patients showed that three quarters of patients rated their care to be good, very good or excellent, although many wished to be more involved in decisions about their own care (Healthcare Commission 2004a). But significantly, the formal evaluation by the Commission for Health Improvement (CHI) commented on a mismatch between official views on meeting targets and user perceptions of the service received (CHI 2003). This suggests there is some 'perception gap' between the service delivered and service as experienced.

This chapter will look at what the Government's prioritisation of mental health has meant in terms of resources, services and policy. Specifically, on policy it looks at public health and the 'personalisation' agenda, which are both areas that are particularly important in relation to mental health.

Resources

One of the most frequently debated issues when it comes to any public service is money: 'Is the Government spending enough?' and 'Is spending likely to increase?' In Europe, mental health problems account for around twenty per cent of total illnesses, and European countries apparently spend between two and thirteen per cent of their health budgets on mental health (McDaid et al 2005).[9]

Compared with other European countries it appears that the UK spends a relatively high proportion of the health service budget on mental health. In 2002–03 around thirteen per cent of the Hospital and Community Health Service (HCHS) budget was spent on mental health. Since 1998-9, spending on mental health has increased in real terms as well, from around twelve per cent to thirteen per cent of HCHS's expenditure.[10] However, there has been a lack of transparency around the additional resources, making it

---

9 As the authors of this study note, twenty per cent is a conservative estimate that does not take into account physical health, mortality or the impact on other family members.
10 HCHS figures provided by the Department of Health. See Rankin 2004 for a more extended discussion of mental health spending.

difficult to assess the impact of increased spending on frontline services (Rankin 2004).

Even more significantly, it is generally agreed that the increase in funding comes from a low base and that mental health has been traditionally under-resourced. In 2001, the Wanless Report stated that 'for too long mental health has been stigmatised and starved of resources and national attention' (Wanless 2001).

Despite some extra resources, mental health trusts are generally below the standards of the average health trust. According to performance ratings of 2004, mental health trusts have the lowest number of three and two star trusts and the highest number of no star trusts, compared with acute trusts, primary care trusts (PCTs), specialist trusts and ambulance trusts (Healthcare Commission 2004b). Notwithstanding ongoing debate over the robustness of the star ratings, it is striking that, even by the Government's own standards, mental health trusts are lagging behind the rest of the health service. In 2003, the CHI considered that historical neglect was still evident in low staff levels, reliance on agencies and poor clinical leadership (CHI 2003). More than half of mental health trusts have had difficulties in implementing their action plans and many cited that these difficulties arose through funding constraints (Audit Commission 2003). Another survey highlighted that staff shortages and inherited debts have held back the development of new services (Sainsbury Centre 2003). In a review of performance on mental health, the Government blamed PCTs for overlooking mental health in favour of clinical services – specifically, this is what the opening quote refers to (DH 2004).

Experts from different perspectives have concluded that mental health is still not the spending priority it should be. On the basis of the Government's spending plans, Derek Wanless argued that mental health spending would need to double by 2010-11 if the Government hoped to deliver on all the objectives set out in the NSF (Wanless 2002). To improve national happiness and wellbeing, Richard Layard has argued the Government may need to spend a higher proportion of the NHS budget on mental health, in particular on treating people with depression, a large group who have been much less visible under recent reforms (Layard 2005b).

Services

In the last two decades mental health services have undergone some substantial changes. Despite this fact, much of the spending on services is directed at a relatively small number of people who are acutely unwell and remains focused on inpatient care. In addition, some of the spending has been criticised because it lacks a sound evidence base and is not always linked to good outcomes for patients. Critics have singled out 'inpatient care, unfocused counselling and unfocused day care' as particular areas for concern (Friedli 2005). This is not unique to English mental health services. Comparative studies suggest that much mental health spending is misdirected (McDaid et al 2005, Lehman et al 2004).

Inpatient care

A significant proportion of the NHS budget for mental health is spent on inpatient care.[11] However, this particular intervention is often ineffective. Experts have described mental health hospitals as providing a 'toxic environment' (McCulloch et al 2003). While there are some good wards, there is also much poorer accommodation, which sometimes exacerbates people's distress. In a survey by Mind, more than half of respondents (fifty-three per cent) commented that a stay in hospital had not helped their recovery, whereas thirty-one per cent of people thought they had become worse as a result. Only one in five people believed they had been treated with dignity and respect (Mind 2004a). In qualitative research with carers who support family members with mental health problems, a further problem was identified, namely that hospitals don't distinguish between the acute and the recovery phases of illness. Carers considered that being around other ill people while in the process of recovery was detrimental to people's prospects for recovery (Rethink 2005).

> Where hospitals fall down at the moment is that even if the psychosis improves they [the service users] are still in that environment and that becomes detrimental to their recovery. (Rethink 2005)

It is well documented that people from BME communities can have a particularly negative experience on inpatient wards. This finding came through strongly in the qualitative work undertaken by the Sainsbury Centre for Mental Health for the report Breaking the Circles of Fear (Keating et al 2004).

One service user remembered first going into hospital: 'I feared that I was going to die.' Another described it as: 'The last straw ... You come to services disempowered already, they strip you of your dignity ... you become the dregs of society.' (Keating et al 2002).

However, research with service users shows that people still want somewhere to go in a crisis, although not necessarily an inpatient ward as they currently operate (Rethink 2005). As one carer puts it: 'We need them for a

---

11 In 2003–04 eighteen per cent of the NHS budget was spent on clinical services mostly comprising inpatient spend. Other major areas of spending are eleven per cent on secure and high dependency provisions, twelve per cent on community mental health teams and twenty-three per cent on indirect investment such as capital charges and overheads (DH 2004).

certain period of time, I don't know what the time is, it's very individual. When a person's in crisis they need to be taken care of.' (Rethink 2005).

Any system will need to offer services to support people in crisis (Thornicroft and Tansella 1999). Evidence on the cost-effectiveness of community and inpatient care suggests that community services do not reduce costs to the health system, but can improve service user satisfaction (McDaid and Thornicroft 2005).

In recent years, there has been a new wave of provision of acute inpatient services, with a general move towards smaller, more domestic-style units. There has also been the development of home treatment teams (Warner 2005). The need for further improvements within inpatient care is recognised by the Government (DH 2004c). Still, the crisis component of services be substantially improved to promote better outcomes, as well as a shift to upstream interventions.

Medication

Medication plays an important role for many people with mental health problems in alleviating symptoms and improving quality of life. It will continue to be an important element of the treatment for some people, alongside other interventions such as psychological treatments and social support. However, there are some significant concerns about how medication is used. In relation to mild mental health problems there are concerns that medication is over-prescribed (House of Commons Health Committee 2005). In relation to severe mental health problems, the concerns centre around a lack of choice and control over medication (Rethink 2005).

In 2003, there were twenty-seven million prescriptions for anti-depressants. From 1991 to 2001 the number of prescription items for all anti-depressants more than doubled in the UK (www.ppa.org.uk). This has been accompanied by a shift in prescribing trends towards SSRIs (Selective Serotonin Reuptake Inhibitors). SSRI prescriptions increased from 8.2 million to more than nineteen million between 1999 and 2003 (MHRA 2003). These trends have prompted growing concern over the medicalisation of society, with increasing numbers of people diagnosed, categorised as abnormal and medicated. Increasingly we live in a world with 'a pill for every ill' (House of Commons Health Committee 2005).

Only five per cent of SSRIs were prescribed for severe depression, with at least two thirds prescribed for people with mild depression. Yet, there is no good evidence that anti-depressants help people with mild depression; they are exposed to a risk of harm with only the prospect of modest benefits (House of Commons Health Committee 2005). Moreover these prescribing levels for mild depression do not fit with National Institute for Health and Clinical Excellence (NICE) guidelines. NICE suggests psychological treatment for mild to moderate depression and psychological treatment in combination with anti-depressants for severe depression (NICE 2004). There is also evidence suggesting that alternative treatments can be at least as effective, for example trials in Germany have shown St John's Wort to be as effective as Paroxetine (an SSRI) in treating moderate to severe depression, and with fewer side effects (Szegedi et al 2005). In fact the success of SSRIs may be purely due to the non-pharmacological response: the person feels better because a doctor's prescription is an official recognition of their unhappiness and they feel hopeful that a formal intervention will restore them. In light of this fact researchers have asked whether pharmacology is 'the most effective, enduring, cost-effective, direct and honest way to deliver such an effect' (The Mental Health Foundation 2005).

Clinical trials show that anti-depressants fail to outperform the placebo. In the United States, analysis of the six most commonly prescribed anti-depressants between 1987 and 1999 showed that, on average, the placebo duplicated eighty-two per cent of the drug response (The Mental Health Foundation 2005). For people with mild mental health problems there is a need to explore alternatives to medication.

In relation to severe mental illness, the issues are somewhat different. For people with serious mental health problems, getting the right medication is can be an important element of the treatment process. Qualitative research with service users shows that people value having control over medication alongside other treatments: for example 'It has to be hand in hand: support, medication, therapy. So as to prevent them [other service users] having a relapse.' (Rethink 2005)

For people with a diagnosis of schizophrenia, NICE guidelines suggest that the new generation of drugs – atypicals – can enable people with schizophrenia to live and work independently. However, there is some evidence to suggest medication is not always prescribed in relation to need. In 2002, NICE noted that many individuals are exposed to unnecessarily high levels of treatment (NICE 2002). According to another account, in 2003 half of all patients taking psychotropic drugs were taking more than one type at a time. Yet there are no studies which have shown the efficacy of taking combinations of these drugs. Some psychiatrists have called into question the 'misplaced therapeutic enthusiasm' for new drugs (Priebe and Slade 2003).

There is also evidence to suggest that some people have little control over their medication. NICE guidelines outline that the choice of anti-psychotic medication should be made jointly by the individual and their clinician. Where possible, clinicians should make use of advance directives to take into account people's wishes (NICE 2002). But many patients receive fairly superficial guidance about their medication, with limited information about side effects or alternatives (Mind 2002). Also, doctors may prescribe without discussing potential side effects that impinge on people's lives. One young woman diagnosed with a severe mental illness recalls the experience of 'being zonked out on high doses of medication which produced severe side effects'. To cope with the side effects she kept stopping the medication and becoming ill again. When given a choice of medication, she opted for something with the side effects least distressing to her (ABPI/LTMCA 2002). However, too few have this level of ownership over their medical treatment or are offered alternatives.

Psychological therapies

Existing resources are disproportionately tied into services where there is some question over their effectiveness. Yet there are large unmet demands for other services, especially psychological therapies.[12] For people with mental health problems, access to psychological therapies is often at the top of their list of priorities (Barnes et al 1999, Wallcraft 2003, Forrest 2004). Not only are talking treatments in demand, but it is also known that, where appropriate, a combination of psychology and drugs is more effective than drugs alone. Therapies such as cognitive behavioural therapy can also help prevent relapses among people with serious mental illnesses (Dickerson 2000).

In comparison with the plethora of targets relating to acute care, there is no target on waiting lists for psychological treatments and hence little public scrutiny of long waiting times. Whilst the average is six to nine months, waiting times of two years have been reported (Forrest 2004, Paxton 2004). Pathways to talking treatments are even harder to access for some groups. Black people with mental health problems are less likely to be offered talking cures, and more likely to be given medication and coercive treatments (Keating et al 2002).

Recently, the Government has begun to address this gap in demand. Over the last decade there has been a significant increase in the number of counsellors in primary care. In recent years the number of psychiatrists and clinical psychologists in the NHS has increased. Between 1999 and 2004 psychiatry consultants (whole time equivalents) increased from around 2,524 to over 3,155, while the number of clinical psychologists increased from 3,763 to 5,331 (DH 2004b). From 2001–02 to 2003–04 there was a real-terms increase in spending on psychological therapies of thirteen per cent (DH 2004c). The Department of Health has written that the future goal is that psychological therapies should no longer be regarded as 'optional' (DH 2004d). The uneven nature of progress shows up in surveys of service users: according to one survey conducted in 2003, access to psychological therapies was rated as one of the top improvements as well as one of the most difficult services to access (Rethink 2003a).

---

12 As defined by the Department of Health (DH 2004d) 'the term psychological therapies covers a wide range of different models, including psychodynamic, cognitive behavioural, arts-based and systemic approaches'.

There is a broader issue here about developing therapeutic relationships. Any expansion in talking therapies needs to happen at the same time as an overall improvement in the quality of people's therapeutic relationships with professionals. Often people with mental health problems may just want someone to talk to. But as some observers have noted, there is a lack of kindness in services (Neuberger 2005).

New services

Much of the reform energy has been directed towards developing new services for mental health. The NHS Plan set out specific targets for crisis resolution teams, assertive outreach teams and early intervention services; services that by 2003–04 represented five per cent of the NHS mental health budget (DH 2004). These bear some of the imprints of the new direction in policy: they are more community-focused, preventative and more personalised. Although it is difficult to offer a definitive judgement on them, there is evidence that they are meeting people's needs in an effective way (Greatley and Ford 2002, Craig et al 2004).

	Number of teams (target figure)	Number of staff in teams	Number of patients covered (target)
Assertive outreach	253 (220)	2,134	13,000 (20,000)
Crisis resolution	174 (335)	2,072	21,000 (100,000)
Early intervention	41 (50)	180	1,900 (7,500)
Total	468 (605)	4,386	35,900 (127,500)

Source: Louis Appleby. Data related to August 2004. Table produced in Layard (2005b).

However, these are highly specialist services, which cover only a small number of acutely unwell people. As the table indicates, in 2004 they supported roughly 35,900 people, with an eventual goal to support 127,500 people.

Large numbers of people with long-term mental health problems do not fall under the remit of these services. Some of them may receive support from a community mental health team. These teams have not received an additional injection of resources, indeed they may have been subject to reduced resources since the creation of specialised services (Burns 2004). Moreover it is likely they have lost trained staff and intellectual capital (Pelosi and Birchwood 2002). It has been considered that these teams, lacking in high profile advocates, find it difficult to meet people's needs (Burns 2004).

The kind of support people would like extends well beyond the traditional remit of services. Surveys by voluntary organisations have pointed out that long-term service users experience poor quality of life, loneliness and isolation (Rethink 2004). The implementation of the NSF has largely been focused on acute services.

> Lack of confidence is my biggest problem. I live in a supported home with other men like me, but I feel lonely and I don't have any friends. Sometimes I go walking by myself, but mostly I stay in bed. *Service user* (Rethink 2004)

> Ten years ago university finished me. I got really ill. It has taken me ten years of medication, yoga classes and sitting in smoking rooms for me now to be left to my own devices. There are endless questions and worries that have been left unanswered and now there is no one to help me get answers. *Service user* (Rethink 2004)

There is a risk that the focus on assertive community services for younger people with more severe problems leads to the development of islands of high quality specialist services among poorer quality routine services. The quality of life of people who have lived with poor mental health for many years has been overshadowed by the drive to create services to help and monitor people who are acutely unwell.

Beyond this group there is a larger number of people with common mental health problems, who have benefited little from mental health's priority status.

Primary care

Around nine in ten mental health problems are treated in primary care, and between thirty and fifty per cent of people with a severe mental health problem only use primary care services (NIMHE 2002). In 2002 primary care received less than ten percent of total mental health spending, and conventionally, it has received much less attention in debates around mental health (Sainsbury Centre 2002). This is changing. The NHS Plan created posts for 1,000 graduate mental health workers to work in primary care and 500 gateway workers to manage transitions between primary and specialist care (DH 2000). The Government has signalled its intention to move mental health reforms into a new phase, from a focus on specialist mental health care towards the health and wellbeing of the whole community (DH 2004). This will require a new approach to mental health and new models for responding to mental health problems.

For most people with a mental health problem, the GP is their first point of contact. In a study of people with severe mental health problems and their carers, people expressed the concern that GPs do not understand mental illness and fail to respond in an effective and timely way

(Rethink 2005). For some people the GP was an obstacle. There were also particular barriers for people from Black and Minority Ethnic communities where language was a problem. One carer pointed out that 'you have to battle your way through the GP before you get anywhere' while another's GP admitted 'we don't have any knowledge of mental health; you have to go to a mental health team'. There were general concerns about communicating with GPs.

> What about those people who can't explain! Some people say their foot hurts or their arm hurts and the doctor will give them medication. But what about those people who can't speak or explain? What can be done about them? *Service user* (Rethink 2005)

For people with common mental health problems, the GP may not be the best point of contact. Relatively few GPs have a special interest in mental health. In one study, three quarters of GPs considered they had either more interest or much more interest in general medicine than psychiatry (Boardman et al 2004).

In a survey by Norwich Union Healthcare of 250 GPs, eight in ten admitted that they were over prescribing anti-depressants and three quarters said they were handing out more of the drugs than they did five years ago (Norwich Union Healthcare 2004). Another national survey showed that ninety-eight per cent of respondents visiting a GP for mental health problems walked out the door with a prescription for medication, even though less than one in five planned to ask for it (Mind 2002).

Policy

Mental health policy has also been affected by some of the wider policy developments across health and social care.

Public health

Recently, public health has been at the forefront of public debate about health policy. The public health 'sins' of smoking, drinking and eating fatty, sugary foods have dominated the headlines and, rightly, captured the interest of policy-makers. Good mental health has not been absent from these debates, but neither has it been central, nor adequately integrated into the bigger picture of the nation's health. In many respects, the national policy framework is supportive of a public health approach to mental health, but there is no overarching strategy to join the different elements together.

The NSF was one of the first major policy documents to outline the importance of mental health promotion, but as yet this has not been central to the delivery of the strategy (DH 1999). Traditionally, spending on prevention and promotion has not been a priority. In 2003–04, the Department of Health spent just 0.07 per cent of the mental health budget on mental health promotion (DH 2004b). Neither has mental health promotion been a priority for researchers and there is a poor evidence base for mental health promotion strategies (McDaid 2005).

In 2004, the Government published a new Public Health White Paper, Choosing Health which outlined its plans for public health (DH 2004b). Mental health and wellbeing is also one of six parts of the Government's strategy on public health, which underlines a commitment to mental health promotion and lists specific initiatives. In addition, the Department of Health has various public service agreement (PSA) targets with the Treasury, which cover reducing mortality rates, narrowing health inequalities and tackling some of the underlying causes of poor health and health inequality. One specific target in relation to mental health is to reduce the suicide mortality rate by twenty per cent by 2010. For many reasons, the suicide rate has been falling in recent years and this goal is on course to be met (DH 2004b). Beyond this, there is a specific target on people with mental health problems.

> Improve life outcomes of adults and children with mental health problems by ensuring that all patients who need them have access to crisis services by 2005 and a comprehensive child and adolescent mental health service by 2006. (DH 2004b).

No one would dispute that these are worthy and important goals. But it is worth asking whether they are enough to promote good mental health and prevent problems before they develop. This focus on prevention can be seen elsewhere in the Public Health White Paper, but is less well defined in relation to mental health. The Public Health White Paper does indicate that there is a plethora of different agencies that contribute to mental and emotional wellbeing: Sure Start, Healthy Schools and Jobcentre Plus. But in a world of competing 'equal priorities' who takes responsibility for good mental health? Does the strategy guarantee coverage for all groups? It is too early to tell, but there is some evidence to suggest that a more co-ordinated strategy is required.

As others have pointed out, under the Public Health White Paper proposals mental health is the only area that lacks a comprehensive strategy for action (Friedli 2005). The mental health of carers also needs to have a more prominent place in the agenda for promoting public mental health and reducing health inequalities (SPRU 2004). Altogether, there appears to be a lack of political leadership, no overarching strategy between the different policy elements, and no clear story to tell about mental health and why it is important.

In Scotland mental health appears to be more integrated into health policy and the work of the Scottish Executive. In 2003 the Scottish

Executive set out a National Programme for Improving Mental Health and Wellbeing. This is designed to raise awareness of mental health issues, eliminate stigma and discrimination, prevent suicide and promote and support recovery. The programme aims to tackle mental wellbeing across the life cycle.

National Programme for Improving Mental Health and Wellbeing

Priority areas:

- Improving infant mental health

- Children and young people

- Employment and working life

- Improving mental health and wellbeing in later life

- Improving community mental health and wellbeing

- Improving local services

(Scottish Executive 2004)

At the time of writing, it is too early to assess the success of the programme, or to judge its impact on mental health in Scotland. Nevertheless, there are several reasons to be optimistic. The programme is based on evidence of what works, including international evidence and pilots. It addresses mental health problems in different places, using a variety of approaches. It has the objective of social participation at its heart. The Mental Health (Care and Treatment) Act 2005 puts a duty on Scottish local authorities to provide services for people with a mental illness, to promote their wellbeing and social development. This includes social, cultural and leisure activities, and training and assistance in finding and maintaining work (TSO 2003). As chapter 4 discusses, the Disability Discrimination Act 2005 is also relevant. This places a positive duty on public authorities to promote equality of opportunity for disabled people. The components of the public health strategy in England and Scotland share some core elements. But what is distinctive about Scotland is the frontline political leadership, overarching coherence of the strategy and the strategy's prominence as part of the work of the Scottish Executive.

Personalised services

Another important policy theme in relation to health policy is the 'personalisation agenda'. Personalisation is a term that covers a broad spectrum of practical realities about involving people in their own care. At one level it covers consultation, for example when users of mental health services are consulted about the day to day management of a mental health trust. On a more ambitious level, personalisation means that users act as 'co-producers' of their own care and are able to take responsibility for determining when and how they are treated. Personalisation is about recognising that the individual brings something to the improvement of their own health. It reorientates the role of professionals from offering 'top down' prescriptions to applying their specific knowledge in a collaborative way (Borg and Khristiansen 2004). In practice, this could mean greater choice for service users in decisions about medication and treatment, or using a direct payment to purchase their own care.

Mental health services appear to have made more progress at the former level, in relation to consulting service users. Many service users do not even have a care plan or a care co-ordinator, let alone a copy of the plan (CHI 2003). The absence of a care plan is symptomatic of the fact that many users are uninvolved with and disengaged from their own care. There is also some ambivalence about choice for people with mental health problems. The Government has been reticent about making the links between choice and mental health (Forrest 2004). At the time of writing, the opportunity to choose between four or five providers does not apply in mental health (DH 2004c).[13] Neither is there an alternative choice for patients who have waited more than six months for treatment, for example for psychological therapies. This extension of choice may be hindered by the absence of waiting list targets for mental health.[14]

The Government has signalled that the lack of choice and personal services needs to change. For example, the long-term conditions framework, which covers people with conditions such as diabetes, multiple sclerosis and mental health problems, outlines that people will have individual care plans and be supported in managing their own care. The Expert Patients Programme is also relevant. Introduced in 2002, this is an NHS-based programme which offers people with long-term conditions self-management courses to enable them to develop skills, confidence and knowledge (www.expertpatients.nhs.uk). On choice, at the time of writing the National Institute for Mental Health in England is exploring ways of extending choice for people with mental health problems.

However, any policy to personalise services will only succeed if it is supported by wider cultural changes within services. Personal services are as much about being treated with dignity and respect, as they are about formal mechanisms such as care plans. Even with the right mechanisms in

13 Specifically, the guidance referred to 'services where other choices are more likely to improve patient experience' (DH 2004d).
14 Most mental health services do not have waiting list targets (Layard 2005b).

place, people can feel alienated if they are not involved in the process of their own treatment. As one carer has said 'They come in, they talk among themselves and they go home again and that's it. You're left on your own again.' The same survey also found that the 'ideal situation is not really something to do with services, but much more to do with recognition and respect.' (Rethink 2005).

The personalisation agenda could be an important force for change in services. Through formal mechanisms, it could help ensure people have greater control and choice over their treatment. Through cultural change it could help promote more collaborative relationships between people and professionals.

* * *

One striking feature of how policy has developed in recent years is that the reforms and new services have grown inside the 'old' system. For instance, despite the evidence on alternatives to medication, for common mental health problems medication remains the default response. Likewise, despite new policy initiatives on public mental health, the system remains focused on treating people in crisis.

Much of the energy behind recent reforms has been directed at the small group of people who are acutely unwell. This has overshadowed efforts to help others with long-term mental health problems or people with more common experiences of depression and anxiety. For all the undoubted and important improvements, most people have seen little change. There has been less effort to meet the needs of people with common mental heath problems, or promote public mental health.

Neither has there has been much progress in improving the life prospects of someone with a serious mental health problem. Mental health reforms have often been pursued in isolation from employment services, social care services or local communities. These are the themes the next chapter will address.

4. Mental health and social inclusion

Mental health problems deny people many opportunities. It has been estimated that someone with a serious mental health problem is four times more likely than an 'average' person to have no close friends (Huxley and Thornicroft 2003). In a survey in 2004, eighty-four per cent of people with mental health problems reported feeling isolated, compared with twenty-nine per cent of the general population (Mind 2004b). These barriers to social networks signal the wider social exclusion of people with mental health problems and there is increasing understanding about the links between poor mental health and social exclusion.

Social exclusion can be defined as a series of interconnected problems around poverty, discrimination, unemployment, low skills, bad housing and poor health. By any account adults with mental health problems are one of the most excluded groups in the UK, while in turn, social exclusion and discrimination sustain poor mental health. As such, it has been argued that social inclusion should be the ultimate goal of a recovery–orientated health service (Sayce 2000).

Despite the well known human and financial costs of mental illness, so far there have been few inroads into the social exclusion and stigmatisation of people with mental health problems. It is worth noting that these policies have also failed to reach some minority ethnic groups. The prospects of a person from an minority ethnic background with a mental health problem are jeopardised by a double burden of disadvantage and discrimination.

This chapter looks at how mental health problems lead to social exclusion and marginalisation for both patients and carers. It does not address all the important areas that are relevant to social inclusion, for example housing. Specifically, the chapter looks at work and meaningful activity. Before turning to these subjects, it is important to consider the foundations that underpin an inclusion agenda: rights, and a new understanding on work and mental health.

Rights and mental health

Rights exist in the overlapping contexts of human rights, civil or political rights and (in an ambiguous way) welfare or social rights (Dean 2002). There is potential for all of these conceptions of rights to have a greater impact on the lives of people with mental health problems. The Human Rights Act 1998 has the potential to shape the provision of public services, for example, by ensuring that services guarantee dignity and respect to the individual.[15] In terms of mental health, the Act has various practical implications, from preventing unnecessary force in secure settings to guaranteeing privacy in hospital wards. However, it has not yet had an impact on the way services are run in the public and voluntary sector (Butler 2004, BIHR 2002).

The Disability Rights Commission (DRC) is playing an important role in enforcing civil/political rights and welfare/social rights, so that people with mental health problems can participate as equal citizens. Its campaigns range from fair treatment at work to equal access to public transport concessions. The DRC aims to challenge the position of mental health as 'the unpalatable face of disability' (DRC 2003). However, it recognises there is not enough awareness among service users about the anti-discrimination provisions of the Disability Discrimination Act 1995. People with mental health problems do not always demand change, because of the associated stigma. Still, in the view of one advocate for change, the Disability Discrimination Act 1995 offers a more powerful tool for change than the more NHS-orientated National Service Framework (NSF) (Sayce 2000). By 2002 twenty-three per cent of all employment cases brought under the Disability Discrimination Act related to people facing discrimination on the basis of mental health, which resulted in a number of high profile cases where individuals secured legal redress (Sayce and Boardman 2003).

The Disability Discrimination Act 2005 places a new duty on public authorities to be proactive about promoting the rights of disabled people. Specifically, public authorities must promote equality of opportunity and positive attitudes towards disabled people. Moreover, and significantly, it brings more people under the remit of the Act, by removing the requirement that mental illness must be 'clinically well-recognised' (TSO 2005).

In bringing mental health into the mainstream there are important lessons to learn from equal rights campaigns led by people with physical disabilities and the Independent Living Movement. The stress on empowered individuals, the importance of making choices, and the centrality of the social model all have resonance for people with mental health problems.

Defining work and meaningful activity

Traditionally work was understood to be full-time, paid employment. It was a view that rendered unpaid commitments in the family or community largely invisible. However, this view has shifted. Increasingly it is accepted that work encompasses other forms of meaningful activity, from unpaid domestic work and caring duties, to voluntary work, as well as part-time and full-time paid work. Meaningful activity itself is even broader, includ-

---

15 The Human Rights Act 1998 guaranteed the freedoms and rights of the European Convention on Human Rights (ECHR) in UK law.

ing education and skills development. But despite our broadening view on work, there remains a need for greater social acknowledgment of the full spectrum of work and meaningful activity. This is necessary if society is to value all contributions.

In the past ippr has argued that we need 'a new account of disability and work' that acknowledges disability as a mainstream issue that affects millions of people. Disability is also a dynamic experience and there is no hard and fast distinction between disabled and non-disabled people (Stanley and Regan 2003).

Within this account there needs to be a better understanding of work and mental health that emphasises rights and recovery. A fact which is often overlooked in the popular discourse on mental health is that the majority of people who experience mental illness can and do recover, although the condition may fluctuate. The term 'recovery' has different meanings in the context of health. In some senses it means a return to wellness. In others, rather than cure, recovery means enabling people as far as possible to live a life on their own terms. As such, a recovery-orientated health system should offer people support in managing mental health problems. For many people, there is no straight road to employment. The nature of mental illness is episodic, and people need support building up to and maintaining work. At the moment the benefits system does not reflect this and making the transition from benefits to work has been likened to jumping off a cliff.

For a minority of people with mental health problems, paid employment will not be appropriate. The Government's focus on employment means less attention has been paid to the needs of people who cannot work at the current time. It is important to start with the presumption that everyone can work and that work takes different forms. But what really matters is some form of meaningful activity: something to do and someone to do it with (Rankin and Regan 2004). Many people with mental health problems want to build up to paid employment by being involved in other forms of meaningful activity, such as voluntary work, education or organised community activities. Ultimately, there are many paths towards recovery.

Employment

Whilst the Government's approach to exclusion has been multifaceted, a key part of the agenda has been based around inclusion through work. The Department for Work and Pensions' Five Year Strategy (DWP 2005) sets out a goal of an eighty per cent employment rate for adults aged sixteen to sixty-four. Achieving this ambitious target will require significant reductions in economic inactivity related to disability. In 2004, there were 2.7 million people claiming Incapacity Benefit (IB); one third of claimants had 'mental or behavioural problems' (DWP 2004).

The Government's aim of increasing the employment rate overlaps with people's own aspirations. People with mental health problems see work as helping them recover an ordinary life. It is clear that participating in work has a therapeutic value, as well as indicating a successful outcome (Boardman 2003).

Yet, there is a substantial gap between people's aspirations and opportunities. Although people with mental health problems have the highest 'want to work rate' among disabled groups, they have the lowest actual work rate. Statistics show that while fifty-two per cent of all disabled people want to work, this figure rises to seventy-eight per cent of people with 'depression and nerves' and eighty-six per cent with 'mental illness, phobias and panics' (cited in Stanley and Maxwell 2004). Evidence from America suggests that between sixty and seventy per cent of people with severe mental illness want to work in competitive employment (Bond et al 2001). However, just twenty-four per cent of people with long-term mental health problems actually do work.

This represents a serious policy problem. It is not a problem of knowledge, as there is evidence about what works. Randomised control studies from the US have shown that the 'place and train model' is more effective than pre-work training in helping people obtain competitive employment, although some people may need time and encouragement to make the transition into paid employment (Crowther et al 2001, Bond et al 2001). If the problem is not evidence, it can be explained by the complex, multiple barriers that prevent people from taking up work. These barriers have been discussed in many accounts (SEU 2004, CAB 2004).

What prevents people working?

- Symptoms of mental illness and side effects of treatment

- Inflexible benefit system

- Individuals' fear of failure and low expectations

- Lack of qualifications due to interrupted education

- Lack of life skills, for example timekeeping and money skills, due to disrupted adolescence

- Stigma and discrimination amongst mental health workforce, as well as employers and society

- Employers' lack of practical knowledge in dealing with mental health problems

- Lack of awareness of rights under the Disability Discrimination Act

- Lack of resources for job brokerage services and job retention support

- Additional barriers: problems posed by lone parenthood or racial prejudice

Here, three reasons are singled out for particular emphasis. These are the benefit system, the historically low priority that has been given to job brokerage services and barriers within the employment market.

Research by ippr has suggested that there is an inconsistency at the heart of IB (Stanley et al 2004, Stanley and Maxwell 2004). On the one hand, an individual must demonstrate their incapacity for work to be eligible for IB; on the other they are required to attend an interview discussing how they might work. This leads to uncertainty, risk aversion and confusion (Stanley et al 2004). People with mental health problems face added difficulties because they may have fluctuating conditions, which the inflexible rules of IB are not always able to accommodate. Permitted work rules are not always well suited to supporting people with mental health problems move into work.[16] The period of fifty-two weeks may be too short for some people to make the transition from permitted work to full-time employment. As such, it can put unnecessary pressure on people to move to full-time employment, and lead to stress, which undermines progress in work and recovery. Furthermore, despite the linking rules permitting people to go back onto benefit at the same rate at which they left benefit, in practice, people have problems getting benefits reinstated (CAB 2004).[17]

Historically, there has been no comprehensive job brokerage system linked to the NHS and social care system. The health and social care system has tended to focus on individual illnesses or problems rather than people's holistic needs. So, despite some important exceptions, the NHS lacks a strong tradition of vocational rehabilitation. Although the NSF suggests implicit support for work, it does not direct emphasis towards employment schemes (Boardman 2003). Outside the NHS, there are government initiatives to promote work for disabled people. These include the New Deal for Disabled people[18] and (the pilots of) Pathways to Work.

Pathways to Work shows the beginnings of a new approach. But historically the size of labour market programmes for disabled people in the UK has been limited. In 2001–02 the UK spent 0.02 per cent of GDP on labour market programmes for all disabled people. This is low compared with other European countries: the EU average was 0.11 per cent, while Sweden, at the top of the table, spent 0.49 per cent (Stanley and Maxwell 2004). The number of occupational therapists also appears to

---

16 Permitted work is allowed for people getting IB in some circumstances: (a) people can earn £20 a week for an unlimited period; (b) people can work for less than sixteen hours a week, with earnings up to £78 a week after deductions, for a twenty-six-week period. This can be extended for a further twenty-six weeks if the person is working with a specified job broker. After fifty-two weeks of permitted work, a further fifty-two weeks must elapse before permitted work can take place again.
17 The linking rules mean that if a person is unable to work within fifty-two weeks of leaving benefits, they may return to them at the same rate as before.
18 The New Deal for Disabled People began in 1998. Participation is voluntary and people are encouraged to contact job brokers at Jobcentre Plus.

be low compared with some other European countries, with one specialist for every 43,000 workers (Henderson et al 2005). Support in employment for people with mental health problems has yet to be attempted on a large scale.

Pathways to Work

The Pathways to Work pilots began in 2003 as a joint programme run by the Department for Work and Pensions and the Department of Health. New entrants to Incapacity Benefit are required to have a series of work-focused interviews with personal advisers to discuss what work they might eventually do. (There are sanctions for non- attendance.) On the health side, people have access to voluntary rehabilitation programmes, focused on helping them to manage their health condition. There are also return-to-work credits for people to help overcome poverty traps. The pilots have been successful: amongst all claimants, there has been a fifty per cent increase in the numbers leaving Incapacity Benefit from the start of the pilots to February 2004. (DWP 2005)

The workplace itself presents multiple barriers to people with mental health problems who want to take up employment. Stigma and discrimination remain common. People with mental health problems are one of the least favoured groups for employment: in 2001 fewer than four in ten employers said they would consider employing someone with mental health problems (SEU 2004).

Traditionally, getting people with mental health problems into work involved getting the person to fit the workplace. Increasingly, a new approach is focused on making the workplace fit the person. At the moment, this approach is observed in theory rather than practice. Most employers do not have a mental health management plan and are not ready to support people with mental health problems. Around half of line managers feel they lack adequate information to manage people with mental health problems (Diffley 2003). Also, some conditions are easier to work with than others.

Community networks

For many people with mental health problems the first step to recovery may precede formal employment, for example developing structured days, through voluntary work or education and training. Organised community networks play an important role in getting people involved in different kinds of meaningful activity and giving them a sense of possibility about the future.

People with severe mental illness are likely to be doing nothing and pass their days in solitary, 'passive leisure' pursuits (Shimitras et al 2003). In contrast, people engaged in structured and creative activity have, on average, fewer readmissions to psychiatric hospitals. There is also evidence to suggest that community interventions and social support networks can be more effective than medication (White and Angus 2003). Service users themselves often stress the importance of neutral spaces and non-medical interventions to improve their mental health. Of a group of service users in touch with Rethink, ten per cent said that better/more personal relationships would be the one thing that would make the most difference to improving their quality of life (Rethink 2003a).

Traditionally, the day centre has been a key social support. It is worth noting that some people who attend day centres think of it as a commitment like work (Catty et al 2001). Day centres have existed for social reasons and offer people the opportunity to participate in creative groups. For some people they become safe havens in an unfriendly world. Early findings from an ethnographic study of people with mental health problems suggest that different organised or informal community networks can become 'safe' places. There is a risk that voluntary social exclusion itself becomes a coping strategy for people on the margins of society (The Living Project Steering Group 2004). Community services tread a fine line between building confidence in a secure environment and presenting people with opportunities to become more involved in mainstream society.

However, the conventional approach to day services has been criticised by campaigners. There is evidence that people's wider needs can be ignored, such as physical health and their aspirations to participate in wider society. At worst, people's recovery is suspended, and they become further adrift from the rest of the community (Clark 2001). Day centres can be predictable and routine: in one survey of time use, people attending day centres had significantly more undescribed time use than average (Shimitras et al 2003). Service users themselves have mixed feelings about day care. Whilst the service is often valued, people are also uncertain about how the services can help with long-term ambitions around recovery and inclusion.

New model of day and community services

- Flexible hours

- Flexible location

- Responsive and adaptable to complex needs

- Culturally and ethnically sensitive

- Supporting people in everyday life and wider integration into the community

- Strong community links

The agenda for modern day services is now concerned with building bridges to the mainstream, rather than simply offering respite or hobbies within the margins of society. There has also been a shift away from buildings. New day services are flexible; they could be in workplaces, health centres or shopping centres. In practice, there are significant variations in modern day/community services. However, there are some common features that could be used to build up a picture of an inclusive day centre. Case studies suggest how they can be orientated to helping people develop structured days and providing social support.[19]

Case study 1: Social Link, north London

Social Link is part of the North London Community Housing Association. It works with clients with severe and enduring mental health problems who are on the Care Programme Approach. At any one time, a team of personal advisers offers 150 people floating support in rebuilding structure into their lives. This includes getting people on training courses or helping people find voluntary work activities that relate to their interests.

Like other day support services, there is an aim to be responsive to people's needs, for example in one case this meant supporting an individual with an interest in horseracing to get work experience at a local race track.

www.communityhousing.org.uk/templates/index.cfm

Case studies suggest that there is no single model for day service provision. What is important is that services are designed and delivered by the local community to meet local needs.

As such, day services cannot afford to become employment bureaux; they need to have a clear mission to support people in all aspects of their lives. However, day services should offer people support and guidance with employment and develop links with local employers. They should be hubs to support meaningful activity in all senses: all kinds of work, social networks and leisure. Jobcentre Plus and Pathways to Work need to ensure that they link effectively with these voluntary services.

Ultimately, the design of the service will depend on what it is trying to achieve. One problematic question is whether day services should have a 'bonding' or a 'bridging' function. In other words should services offer people with mental health problems a haven to share experiences, or

---

19 The Social Exclusion Unit (SEU 2004) report contains many interesting and instructive case studies. The decision was taken not to reproduce these examples.

Case study 2: Resource, Reading

The Reading Mental Health Resource Centre offers its members work opportunities, support and training for paid work, as well as a place to socialise and meet people. There is a deliberately small number of paid staff, so the centre relies on paid and voluntary members to plan and run the service. Resource also aims to make connections with groups who may not ordinarily come into contact with the service, such as African-Caribbean people with mental health problems.

Resource was founded in 2001 and has over 600 members. Since 2001 more than forty-eight people have returned to paid work and eighty people have taken up internal employment, with many others participating in training programmes and social activities.

www.resource.uk.net

should they offer a bridge to the mainstream community? It is likely that both will be relevant for different people with different experiences of mental health problems, but in the long run, day centres cannot afford to reinforce people's social exclusion. Even 'voluntary' social exclusion needs to be challenged, because it has negative repercussions for social solidarity and welfare (Le Grand 2003).[20] Community networks need to develop

Case study 3: 999 Club, Deptford

The 999 Club offers friendship, help and advice to disadvantaged people in south London. From one building in Deptford, the club offers facilities that are open to the whole community, including a café as well as dance, exercise and relaxation classes. Beyond this, it takes referrals from GPs, community mental health teams, hospitals, the police, prisons, courts and other agencies to provide support for people with varying levels of complex needs, such as mental health problems, substance misuse and poverty.

It was started in 1992 and offers both immediate help with any situation and long-term support. It is staffed by local people and helps over 1,000 people a year, with the community as a whole also making use of the facilities.

www.999club.org/index.htm

20 For further discussion on the life choices and voluntary social exclusion see Rankin (2005b).

strategies to help people move on from 'safe places' into the mainstream community.

Carers

Carers are also disadvantaged in employment. In 2003, two thirds of carers of working age were in paid employment, and of these, one fifth provided more than twenty hours of unpaid care in the home (Evandrou and Glaser 2003). Despite the number of people this covers, working arrangements can be insufficiently flexible to enable carers to undertake paid work. For instance, one third of female carers could not readjust their work hours after their caring stopped or changed (Evandrou and Glaser 2003). These problems continue despite the fact that carers' needs are often very simple. In one survey of mental health carers in Somerset people wanted guarantees of being able to leave work on time, opportunities to call home to reassure themselves and more advice on balancing employment and caring (Ogilvie 2003).

Measures to promote social inclusion of service users and carers

The Government needs to continue to focus on promoting the social inclusion of people with mental health problems and carers.

Incapacity Benefit

Elsewhere, ippr has recommended comprehensive reforms to the current system of Incapacity Benefit (IB) by replacing it with an Earnings Replacement Allowance (ERA).[21] This would uncouple incapacity from disability by indicating a replacement basic income, rather than a payment for health problems or disability. Such a reform seems particularly appropriate for mental health, where many people want to work. ERA would be paid at a flat rate, which would help clear the existing confusion around the linking rules. This would also make the move into work feel less risky (Stanley and Maxwell 2004).

The ERA would need to be more responsive to the particular issues around mental health than IB has been. It would need to take better account of the fluctuating nature of mental health problems. Permitted work rules could be adapted so that people are able to do part-time work and be eligible for certain benefits beyond a period of fifty-two weeks. In this more flexible model, the benefit system would be more like a staircase, which people can go up and down, rather than a cliff, from which people can have trouble returning to benefits. The Disability Rights Commission

---

21 See Stanley and Maxwell (2004) for a full discussion of the ERA and its proposed advantages over the current IB arrangements.

has proposed moving away from a system of waivers and permissions for certain disabled people towards 'structural reasonable adjustment', promoting activities that help individuals to fulfil obligations (Howard 2004). The pathway back to work would vary according to each individual's problems and existing skills. This demands a highly personalised system of job brokerage, where job advisers work with people on a case by case basis to plan the best route to work.

At the time of writing, the Government has proposed reforms to out-of-work benefits. It is planned that IB will be replaced with new arrangements for out-of-work benefits, which will be more focused on what people can do. It is expected that the system will be in place for new claimants by 2008 (DWP 2005).

A comprehensive job brokerage system

The National Institute for Mental Health in England is charged with working towards the goal of a personal employment adviser for everyone with severe mental illness. This is an important ambition for services, but is likely to require new resources in order to train job brokers and NHS staff. It has been estimated that it would cost £500 million to roll out the Pathways to Work pilot scheme (which covers all disability) on a national scale (Stanley and Maxwell 2004). The Pathways to Work pilot scheme is a promising model, because it includes access to a personal adviser, work-readiness support and support in employment. Service users and carers echo the need for two stages of support, to get into work and to stay in work.

> I think there's a need for a sort of midwife, first to gain the employment and then to marry the gap between the non-working condition, and then once in employment there is a need for a counsellor or buddy there. *Carer* (Rethink 2005).

As noted, the Pathways to Work pilots have proved to be successful and this approach is set to be extended. For people with mental health problems, there needs to be particular attention to ensuring that people feel comfortable in engaging with the work-focused interview process and have the appropriate support to do so. Confidence in Employment (see case study 4) suggests how one kind of work-readiness support works in practice.

The issue of tackling discrimination in the workplace is also critical to helping people with mental health problems stay in work.

An adequately funded programme to promote anti-discrimination and practical knowledge in employment

The Government has highlighted tackling stigma as an important part of the strategy for mental health (SEU 2004, DH 1999). A key component of this strategy needs to be a programme directed towards employers and the workplace. However it is important not to bundle all problems into the bracket of stigma (though this issue is undoubtedly important). Some issues are as basic as a lack of information and practical support. Discussions with people involved in community projects indicate that new employers need more facts about mental health and practical information on supporting people at work. Some practical steps include wider dissemination of guidance on mental health, such as the Line Manager's Guide to Mental Health produced by Mind Out for Mental Health. Guidance should include advice on what might constitute reasonable adjustments under the Disability Discrimination Act. Clients on supported employment schemes have found that helpful reasonable adjustments were flexible hours and patterns of work (Secker 2000).

Case study 4: Confidence in Employment at Rethink East Midlands Project Office

Confidence in Employment is one element of the Pathways to Work pilot in Derbyshire. People who are registered on the pilot attend a compulsory meeting with an Incapacity Benefit personal adviser. They have access to cognitive behavioural therapy, as well as other services to help manage their lives.

One service which people can be referred to is Confidence in Employment. This is a voluntary, six day course over three weeks, which is designed to help people prepare for employment. It is aimed at people with 'mild to moderate mental health problems', although in practice this definition covers a wide variety of experiences. The course focuses on helping people manage their mental health problems and prepare for employment. It introduces people to volunteering and also helps them to balance work with other activities such as exercise and a social life. Described as 'helping people to speak for themselves', it aims to develop lateral thinking, self-esteem and assertiveness. It helps individuals find ways to present mental health problems, for example thinking about appropriate language and strategies when discussing mental health with employers.

Better support for carers

Across government, there needs to be greater recognition of the contribution of informal care. The new services for carers, such as care plans, have had some impact. In one survey of carers, forty-seven per cent thought that carers' support services had improved (Rethink 2003b). However, this impact may be blunted as care policies have not been fully supported by broader changes to the health, tax and benefit system. Neither is their parity of esteem for caring alongside paid employment. There is a need for a complete and visible strategy on carers' needs. In particular, solutions need to focus on those carers who provide a significant number of caring hours in a week.

Caring as a tax and benefit issue

Recognising the contribution of unpaid caring through the tax and benefit system would help to contribute to a fairer deal for carers. At the moment only carers caring for thirty-five hours a week are entitled to pension credits. It has been argued that extending tax and pension credits to those caring for sixteen hours a week needs to be considered on the grounds of equity (Evandrou and Glaser 2003).

Support strategies in the workplace

Carers could be better supported in the workplace, through provisions such as the right to request flexible working and compassionate leave. Such provisions could be contained in better guidance for employers about reasonable adjustments for carers. At the time of writing, the Department for Trade and Industry (DTI) is consulting on extending the right to request flexible working arrangements for new groups of people, including people who care for ill or disabled adults (DTI 2005). Carers' support plans also need to help people combining work and caring. For instance, they may need to focus more on offering practical help, such as help with shopping.

* * *

What happens if we do not pursue social inclusion? Without serious efforts to promote social inclusion, people with mental health problems are likely to remain marginalised at the edges of society. Mental health will continue to exact heavy costs on individual lives and financial costs on government. In contrast, progress on all indicators of exclusion promises a reduction in misery due to mental health problems and could help shape a more socially cohesive society.

In the light of the Social Exclusion Unit report (SEU 2004), it is a promising time for change. Of course, it would be naïve to expect government alone to achieve inclusion. Local communities, the media, private and voluntary sectors and private individuals all play a role in determining the success of social inclusion. However, much will depend on government policies and how they are implemented.

Part 3
The way forward

5. A vision for mental health

The development of mental health policy over the last decade shows that there are different visions about the future of mental health. At various times, policy-makers have emphasised rights and inclusion, as well as risk management and public safety. The role of mental health has been neglected in the debates around public health. From the top levels of government, there has been no clear and consistent narrative about mental health. While politicians feel confident discussing the future of the NHS and the importance of good physical health, it is extremely rare to hear a politician articulate a vision for good mental health. It is rarer still for it to be reported in the national media.

Nevertheless, if society's response to mental health is going to change, as it must, there needs to be a clear vision to underpin interventions and services, as well as public understanding. This chapter offers this vision and sets out five themes to underpin future mental health policy:

- targeted universalism

- public health

- social inclusion

- rights-based mental health

- personalisation

Targeted universalism

Mental health is a universal good. It has been described as a resource, 'a value on its own and as a basic human right essential to social and economic development' (WHO 2004a). Underpinning good social relationships, health and quality of life, it is something to be valued by individuals, communities and policy-makers. It is not the sole business of the NHS or specialist services, but a responsibility shared across all public agencies.

As such, mental health policy needs to be designed to meet the needs of the whole population, focusing on all age groups. Policy-makers need to provide leadership in ensuring that good mental health is universally valued and universally supported. In particular, local government, with its wide remit for community wellbeing, has an important role to play in creating the right conditions for good mental health to flourish.

Yet, within a universalist focus there needs to be specific support to improve the mental health of people with serious mental health problems and those who are most at risk of poor mental health. People with serious mental health problems are likely to be poor and excluded on many different levels. There needs to be a particular focus on improving their life outcomes. People from poor backgrounds face a slightly higher risk of poor mental health and are more likely to find it difficult to access services – the 'inverse care law'. Of course, strategies to end poverty and deprivation should also help to improve mental health, for example, if the Government meets the pledge to end child poverty by 2020 this should contribute to better mental health. Nevertheless, there is a need to develop particular strategies to improve mental health in deprived areas.

A framework of targeted universalism is consistent with the reforms that are unfolding in social care. For example, Children's Trusts will offer high quality universal services for all children, with specific interventions to help those children at risk. The Green Paper on adult social care outlined a vision where care is part of the social fabric and local commissioners have a complete picture of local need, but where services and support are targeted at those most in need (DH 2005c). To date, the universal element has been missing from mental health policy.

One development that ought to be significant is that in 2005 the UK was among the fifty-two states of the European region of the WHO that signed up to a declaration on mental health. This set out five priorities for the next ten years, with the first priority to foster awareness of the importance of mental wellbeing (www.euro.who.int). This also provides an agenda for setting out mental health as an issue to be universally supported.

Public health

The case for prevention rather than cure has long been a feature of the public health debate in relation to physical health. It is now becoming equally salient for mental health and wellbeing. The WHO has shown that mental health prevention (preventing symptoms of mental health problems and disorders) and mental health promotion (promoting good mental health) can have an impact in improving health and reducing costs to governments (WHO 2004a, WHO 2004b).

One study has found that around a quarter of cases of schizophrenia and a quarter of cases of adult depression could be prevented through a well-timed intervention in childhood (Kim-Cohen et al 2003). Treating and preventing symptoms of depression can reduce the risk of a major depressive episode (WHO 2004a). The overlap between mental health and physical health problems suggests the need for integrated public health policies, targeting particular groups and particular problems.

Public agencies need to develop policies to prevent mental health problems and promote good mental health, which are integrated across public services. In some areas, such as schools and the early years, there is an infrastructure in place, for example the Healthy Schools Initiative and Sure Start. As has been discussed, mental health is part of the Government's strategy on public health. However, it has been noted that mental health is the only part of the Government's public health strategy which does not include a range of specific initiatives to reduce prevalence, especially in the context of inequalities (Friedli 2005). There is a need for an ambitious public health strategy, to help move towards an environment where people are encouraged to seek help early.

Social inclusion

Part of the core business of mental health services should be supporting people in living their lives, and promoting their opportunities and inclusion in wider society. The Government has produced strong statements of its intention to pursue the social inclusion of people with mental health problems and other disabilities (Strategy Unit 2005, SEU 2004).

> By 2025, disabled people in Britain should have full opportunities and choices to improve their quality of life, and will be respected and included as equal members of society. (Strategy Unit 2005).

This strategy will be driven forward by a new Office for Disability Issues, reporting to the Minister for Disabled People. Many people with long-term mental health problems would not think of themselves as disabled, but they fall under the provisions of the Disability Discrimination Acts (1995 and 2005).

The Social Exclusion Unit's strategy on mental health and inclusion is wide-ranging, covering the role of health and social care, employment, supporting families, housing and transport, and implementation (SEU 2004). A central part of this strategy is challenging stigma and discrimination, especially in the media. The more adults who are able to participate in mainstream activities and disclose their condition, the easier it will be to overcome stereotypes. As has been argued, societies that stigmatise mental health problems tend to get the very problems they fear: those which are hidden and unpredictable (Smith 2002).

It is important to remember that social marginalisation affects people who care for people with a long-term disability or health problems. Carers need to be part of the wider strategy on social inclusion. People who spend a high proportion of time caring for relatives have needs for greater support in their caring role, such as respite care. Beyond caring, there is a need for recognition of people's caring responsibilities in employment to help people balance their work and home responsibilities.

Rights-based mental health

Social inclusion is most likely to succeed if it is underpinned by a rights-based approach. A rights-based approach has moral authority; it does not depend on understanding, familiarity or good feeling towards individuals (Smith 2002). Moreover, rights are a practical tool and people can get redress in a court of law. As well as legal redress, rights can create a new culture of expectations about what people can expect and what they can contribute.

The Human Rights Act is one tool to establish a rights-based approach to mental health. The rights provided under the Human Rights Act are guaranteed to everyone, but are especially important to protect vulnerable people. Human rights legislation provides an enforceable system for protecting people who have experienced maltreatment and discrimination. It is particularly important for people who are compulsorily detained under the provisions of the Mental Health Act. Traditionally this has meant an erosion of people's personal rights and freedoms, in very basic things such as eating, drinking and daily routine (Mental Health Taskforce 2003). The legislation needs to become embedded in the day-to-day working practices of inpatient wards or their future equivalents. The development of a 'culture of human rights' could help shift the balance from viewing people as patients to viewing them as citizens.

The Disability Discrimination Acts will continue to play an important role. For instance, someone with a severe mental illness denied time to explain their needs in a bank or shop, or who was given a lower quality of physical healthcare than other patients could bring a challenge under the Act. Advocates of the Disability Discrimination Act (DDA) 2005 have argued that it is important that psychiatrists let service users know that they have the right to be served equally in public places and when accessing public services (Sayce and Boardman 2003). This also applies to other professionals working with people with mental health problems, such as nurses and workers in the voluntary sector. All professionals working with people with mental health problems need to have knowledge of people's rights.

The DDA 2005 fills in some of the gaps of the DDA 1995. As the last chapter noted, the new Act is significant in that more people fall under its remit as the requirement for mental health problems to be 'clinically well-recognised' has been removed (HMSO 2005).

In future the single equalities commission[22] should play an important role in helping to deliver rights, especially for people facing complex dis-

---

22 A single equalities commission will take the place of three bodies that challenge discrimination. The Commission for Equality and Human Rights (CEHR) will bring together the work of three existing equality commissions – the Commission for Racial Equality, the Equal Opportunities Commission and the Disability Rights Commission.

crimination and exclusion, for example a black person with mental health problems who was unfairly discriminated against. The Commission for Equality and Human Rights will reflect people's complex overlapping identities. But there is a need to ensure that different anti-discrimination agendas are given equal weight. Mental health service users and carers believe it would help if discrimination on the grounds of mental health was pursued with the same determination as other forms of discrimination, for example 'making mental health the same high profile issue as racism [or prejudice against] homosexuality' (Rethink 2005).

More and more, we hear 'responsibilities' presented as the rhetorical balance to 'rights'. In relation to mental health, responsibility is an important theme. In the past, the 'stigma of benevolence' – the assumption that people are incapable – proved to be just as damaging to people with mental health problems as the stigma of violence (Sayce 2004). For example, in the workplace, people with mental health problems who have been given too little responsibility or too small a workload can feel undermined, despite an employer's best intentions (Sayce and Boardman 2003). There needs to be greater recognition of people with mental health problems as contributors to families, workplaces and communities. As has been noted, full citizenship requires individuals to carry the same responsibilities as others, but this entails making reasonable adjustments and providing support to enable people to meet their responsibilities. As Howard notes, 'Rather than rights being conditional on responsibilities having been met, additional needs have to be identified and met beforehand (rather than the other way round)' (Howard 2004).

Policy-makers need to begin from the starting point of what people can do and how they can contribute. On this score, there are promising signs from Government. Policy statements have discussed, ending a culture of low expectations of people with disabilities (DH 2005a, Strategy Unit 2005). Similarly, some new policy initiatives are based on a new understanding of people's capabilities. The approach of the Pathways to Work pilots marked a new approach in changing perceptions of the advisers and health professionals, which have traditionally been low (Howard 2004).

This kind of approach suggests an attempt to move away from a culture based around exaggerated ideas of risk. A focus on managing risk has been particularly damaging for people with mental health problems. Organisations including the Royal College of Psychiatrists and the Disability Rights Commission have argued that a threshold of 'capacity' should be used, with only those demonstrably lacking capacity being treated without consent (Sayce 2004). This was not the approach taken by the Government when it introduced the proposals for the new Mental Health Bill between 2002 and 2004, which were based around compulsory treatment in the community. These elements were rejected by the Mental

Health Scrutiny Committee, which recommended that patients should never be treated under compulsion unless their decision making capacity is impaired, and that any compulsory treatment must be appropriate (Joint Committee 2005). These recommendations are more in line with a rights-based citizenship approach.

Personalisation

It is difficult to generalise about mental ill-health, although the traditional approach from services has been based on broad, undifferentiated responses. Ultimately, there is no single intervention that will successfully improve mental health for every person in every context. However, there is a significant amount of evidence about what works, which unfortunately has not always been reflected in the allocation of resources or day-to-day practice.

One aspect of a more personalised approach to mental health problems is to enable people to have more choice and control over treatment. The third working paper of this project made a case for why choice could produce better outcomes for people with mental health problems and could lead to better allocation of resources (Rankin 2005a). Choice in mental health is different to how the policy has developed in the rest of the health service. Choice in a consumerist sense – the opportunity to choose different providers – has a less central role. Discussions with service user groups indicate that people are more concerned about access to services and choice of key worker, rather than 'consumer choices' (Barnes et al 1999).

People who have experienced moderate to severe mental health problems identified the opportunity to have control and make choices as a major factor in the maintenance of their mental health (Faulkner 2000). A choice of treatments should be available because it would help to maximise treatment response.

> [a] wide array of effective treatments should be available within a community, because even when treatments are equally effective on average, many of them are not equally effective for significant sub-groups. (Lehman et al 2004).

Choice holds out the prospect of more effective, more efficient services that are aligned to the interventions that work for individuals. In this context, choice is also an end in itself and could help to reinforce other agendas on rights and social inclusion. If society reaches a stage where people have a choice in treatment, but no choice in life decisions, such as employment or education, the choice agenda could be judged to have failed. Choice is part of a larger agenda of social inclusion for people on the margins of society. Without steps towards greater social inclusion, people's life choices will be empty.

Alongside choice, there need to be more individualised responses to people with mental health problems. Health and social care services need to take greater account of the complexity of people's lives, and the experiences and aspirations that fall outside the boundaries of conventional services. As one person described it, services need to:

> look ... at the whole pattern of a life, what interests have you got, how can we help ...and also look ... at their point of view. What interests do they really want to pursue? *Carer* (Rethink 2005)

More personal and therapeutic relationships could help to achieve a significant improvement in how people are treated. On one level therapeutic relationships could mean an expansion of talking treatments, but equally, it could be as simple as promoting better personal relationships between service users and professionals, in which people are respected and have someone to talk to. One person recalls a helpful relationship with a psychologist: 'I could talk about anything ... everyday life things that were important to me, not necessarily problems ... I was the one who decided what to talk about' (Borg and Kristiansen 2004). As this suggests, good patient-professional relationships are non-procedural, based on empathy and mutual respect. Developing a health system where these therapeutic relationships are routine needs to happen alongside any expansion in provision of services for people with mental health problems.

* * *

Elements of all these principles are already present in some form, in some aspects of policy or services. Notably, social inclusion is at the forefront of policy, although this has raised concerns that its prominence is at the expense of broader public health objectives (Friedli 2005). But policy-makers need to have a co-ordinated strategy on mental health, with all these themes in mind. This suggests that what could be new is the combination of all these elements as a positive narrative about mental health.

In total, these themes could help to shape a new narrative about mental health. Policy-makers need to use such a narrative to help create a more mental-health literate society. This will require some specific interventions, including targeted interventions to schools, the public sector and the media in the context of a sustained national programme for mental health and wellbeing. Many of the building blocks are in place, but there is an important role for local and central government in offering leadership with conviction and a coherent sustained strategy for better mental health.

6. Policy recommendations

Mental health problems are inextricably linked to many complex social problems, including poverty, worklessness and social exclusion. Clearly, there are large areas of policy that have or could have an impact on the population's mental health. For example, the Government's commitments on poverty reduction and citizenship for disabled people might be expected to have a positive impact on the nation's mental health.

This report focuses on key changes in the health and social care system that would improve outcomes for people with mental health problems. Altogether, public policy might look very different if it was focused on promoting mental health.

In part A, this chapter sets out six key recommendations for public policy.

1 A renewed focus on primary care and community health

2 A role for access workers

3 The development of Community Health Centres

4 Improved access and provision of non-pharmacological treatments

5 Pilots of personal recovery budgets

6 Refocusing of inpatient care

These recommendations should be read in conjunction with the recommendations on social inclusion set out in chapter 4.

But a prescription for change is not enough. Therefore part B offers some consideration on how to overcome barriers to change. In particular it looks at issues around resources, systems and structures, commissioning, service user involvement, culture change and political ownership.

Part A

(1) A renewed focus on primary care and community health
Community-orientated primary care should be the main driver in improving mental health services and the mental health of local communities. The reasons for focusing on primary care are clear: primary care is already the place where most mental health issues are seen; recently, primary care has assumed new responsibilities for providing and commissioning services. A new focus on community-orientated primary care would help to rebalance the health system towards more common mental health problems, as well

as help provide better quality of support for people with long-term mental health problems. The Government has already stated its intention to turn the spotlight of reform onto primary care (DH 2004c). However, much will depend on the nature of the reforms and the political commitment behind them.

Since 1997, there has been a significant increase in the number of integrated community initiatives, such as Healthy Living Centres, the New Deal for Communities, Sure Start and Local Strategic Partnerships. There has also been interest in new types of professionals who broker services and support people in achieving healthy lifestyles. ippr has recommended the development of service navigators, lead professionals to support people in accessing services and developing a complex care package (Rankin and Regan 2004). The Public Health White Paper, Choosing Health, has set out a vision for 'health trainers', who could work with people to help develop self-sustaining healthy lifestyles (DH 2005a).

For mental health, there needs to be a similar approach. This report argues that a new approach to primary care needs to focus on:

- access workers
- Community Health Centres

(2) A role for access workers

For most people who experience mental health problems, the GP is the main point of contact and the main gatekeeper to other services. While there are many GPs who are effective in this role, this system does not seem to work for most people most of the time (as discussed in chapter 3). This is true both for people with severe mental illness and those with common mental health problems.

In order to improve primary care, this report proposes the introduction of access workers. These may be professionals with a medical background, such as GPs with a special interest in mental health, nurses or health visitors. They may also be people from grassroots community organisations, who have appropriate training. The access worker would be able to act as a service navigator, to help people negotiate public services and get the right interventions and support in relation to their mental health.

Access workers would be able to offer everything from a friendly ear to professional counselling, as well as offering an entry route to other talking treatments, local support groups, medication and sport or art on prescription. They would be trained to recognise the symptoms of mental health problems, but would not offer people a formal diagnosis. These different professionals could be based in a variety of mainstream community locations, such as Children's Centres, community centres, GPs' surgeries and libraries. Where appropriate locations did not exist, access workers could be based in new types of community organisations, such as Connected Care Centres (Rankin and Regan 2004) or Community Health Centres.

(3) Community Health Centres

One of the historical problems with mental health provision is that mental health problems are treated as medical problems, a view that overlooks their social causes and social consequences. This view is changing (SEU 2004), but could be strengthened by developing integrated community initiatives to meet mental health needs.

In the past ippr has recommended the model of Connected Care Centres to provide social support to people in deprived neighbourhoods (Rankin and Regan 2004). This model is designed to ensure health and social-care support for people with complex needs, who traditionally have fallen between the gaps in services. Connected Care Centres are based on common principles, rather than a fixed specification and the model will vary according to local needs. This is part of the Government's vision for the future of social care (DH 2005c).

Connected Care Centres

- Co-location of NHS, social care and voluntary sector professionals

- Common assessment procedure

- Established procedures for sharing information

- Shared training

- Single point of entry

- Round-the-clock support

- Managed transitions – flexible approach to age boundaries

- Continuing support – no 'closed cases'

(Rankin and Regan 2004)

It was envisaged that Connected Care Centres would be based in deprived neighbourhoods. However, many of the principles could have a more universal application in promoting the health and mental health of all local communities. Community Health Centres would be able to support people in all aspects of a healthy life, both mental and physical. Again, there is no fixed blueprint for the model, but a set of common features.

Community Health Centres would offer people a neutral, non-medical space, something that many people with long-term mental health problems

Community Health Centres

- Co-location of different NHS, social care and voluntary sector professionals

- Being visible in the community and easy to access

- Offering established routes into specialist services and a single point of entry into other services

Specifically, for people with mental health problems they could:

- offer advice and support in the first instance

- facilitate access to specialist health services if appropriate, or other public services including employment, education and careers advice, leisure and housing

- advise family and friends who may be concerned about helping someone with a mental health problem

- advise employers on anti-discrimination legislation relating to mental health, such as reasonable adjustments

- offer social prescriptions, such as 'bibliotherapy' (books on prescription) or exercise on prescription, but not any pharmacological prescriptions

- provide connections to other community support groups and networks based in the community

- help people to manage their own health and mental health

- run courses, for example on self-management of long-term conditions or returning to work for people who have been unemployed or on Incapacity Benefits

value (Wallcraft 2003). The Centres could also be hubs of information, supporting people to 'self help' on all health problems. Qualitative research has consistently shown that people with mental health problems want information.

> When I was first diagnosed as being depressed I wanted to find out all about it and read as much as I could, to find out why and what caused it and what would help that sort of thing. I think it is important. For some people just writing and asking for information about depression and where they can go to get help, is actually just a small step to helping. It might be all they need. (Faulkner 2000)

Community Health Centres could also be places for people with long-term conditions to get advice and resources to manage their conditions. The Centres would need to build links with established initiatives, such as the Expert Patients Programme. Among people with long-term mental health problems, there is demand for support with self-management. In focus groups, people with mental health problems talked about places where there were opportunities to learn about mental health: 'We need a community-based centre where we can go and learn these things [mental health issues]. But there are none. They need to be made' (Rethink 2005).

One service user from research conducted for this project offered a definition of self-management:

> Sort of looking at yourself, learning about yourself, and actually seeing right in a crisis... [asking] 'how d[id] I actually get here', look at it ... [and] be aware [that] this is what is happening. (Rethink 2005)

Community Health Centres would be a place for family members to go if they had concerns about a relative's mental health. This could be particularly important for people who care for family members with severe mental health problems or other long-term health problems. At the Community Health Centres they would be able to get information about supporting the person they are caring for, as well as advice on strategies for coping. This was one theme that was highlighted by carers in qualitative work carried out by Rethink.

> Take away the mystique of who these dual diagnosis people are and tell us how they are handling it, give us some of those skills, empower us with knowledge. (Rethink 2005)

As well as support on caring, these Centres would also help carers manage their own health problems or concerns.

This model of Community Health Centres is not dissimilar to other integrated community-based initiatives, for example Children's Centres. Community Health Centres would function in a similar way, being integrated and locally developed. It is envisaged that they would be local hubs of knowledge and expertise on good health, as well as providing a complete approach to meeting physical and mental health needs.

(4) Improve access and provision of non-pharmacological treatments

If the agenda of community-based mental health is to be successful, it will require some basic changes in the provision of mental health resources. After all, if there is a new kind of access worker there need to be appropriate services that people can access. As discussed in chapter 4, there needs to be particular focus on developing non-pharmacological treatments. Of course, for some people, medication will continue to play an important role as part of the treatment package. But everyday practice needs to become consistent with National Institute for Health and Clinical Excellence (NICE) guidelines, which show that medication needs to be used in the right way at the right time (NICE 2004, NICE 2002). Medication needs to take its place as an element of treatment, rather than the whole treatment.

Psychological Therapies

There is overwhelming evidence that people with all kinds of mental health problems want to access psychological therapies (see chapter 3). People should be able to choose between different types of evidence-based psychological therapy. This would require an increase in the number of specialists. Richard Layard has advocated a goal of 5,000 more cognitive behavioural therapists over a Parliament, as well as doubling the number of training places for clinical psychiatrists (Layard 2005b). In the first instance, these professional services should be available to people with psychosis and severe depression, which would bring current practice in line with NICE guidelines.

Psychological treatments should be subject to waiting lists, with corresponding targets and political pressure to reduce waiting times. A target on waiting times would be valuable in concentrating energies and resources on improving access to psychological therapies, which remains very uneven. But mental health services need to learn lessons from acute healthcare on using targets in a sensitive way to minimise the risk of perverse incentives. As the debacle over booking GP appointments demonstrated in 2005, targets can be a blunt instrument. They need to be used sensitively, bearing in mind the overall objectives of the service.

In order to build capacity within mental health services, mental health policy-makers could look to the example of what happens elsewhere in the NHS. Some mental health organisations have put forward the idea of diagnostic and treatment centres for mental health (Sainsbury Centre 2003). If people are able to access the support they need, free at the point of use, it will be unimportant whether those services are supplied by the public or private sector.

However, given the inevitable limits on resources, not everyone with mental health problems will be able to see a psychiatrist or psychologist – nor would they necessarily want to. In the first instance, there is also a need for people with counselling skills for more common mental health problems, which could be provided by access workers. If appropriate, these access workers would be able to help people access mental health specialists.

It is also worth remembering that what many people want is simply someone to talk to and a better quality of therapeutic relationships with professionals. An expansion in the provision of talking therapies needs to take place alongside a wider cultural change in health services, in which people with mental health problems are treated with kindness and respect.

Social Prescribing

There is a clear need to develop knowledge about and capacity for social prescriptions, such as exercise on prescription, or books or art on prescription. There are numerous examples of innovative local services, many of which are described in the Social Exclusion Unit report (SEU 2004). PCTs need to develop links with and support existing user-led organisations, such as time banks, reading schemes or music groups. There is a need to develop a stronger evidence base in relation to arts therapies, as there is no quantitative work on the possible health benefits (White and Angus 2004). The Mental Health Foundation has published evidence on the positive effects of sport and is leading a campaign to promote the benefits of exercise of prescription (Mental Health Foundation 2005).

Stockport Arts and Health

In the early 1990s, Stockport Arts and Health pioneered arts on prescription, arranging referrals from GPs or other health workers to local arts organisations. Results from a small sample found a reduction in the number of participants with a recognisable mental health problem. (White and Angus 2003)

Rushey Green Time Bank, Catford

Rushey Green Time Bank was developed by local GPs and the New Economics Foundation to tackle depression. Set up in 2000, it aims to build capacity and support networks in the local community. It is part of a wider network of London Time Banks, which operate on a 'parallel economy', where time is the main unit of exchange. They attract people who are normally the recipients of volunteering, rather than the volunteers. An evaluation of Rushey Time Bank suggests that it has contributed to building confidence and self-esteem and has reduced visits to the GP. www.londontimebank.org.uk

(5) Pilots of personal recovery budgets

The NHS has often proved fairly unresponsive to people's demands for different kinds of services, notably talking treatments. Introducing greater individual budget-holding, through direct payments, could help to remedy this. If people were given their own personal recovery budget they could choose their own treatment (Rankin 2005). This would also help correct a theoretical anomaly where people (at least, those who are eligible for community care) have choice in social care, but not in healthcare.

A personal recovery budget is, in essence, a direct payment for mental health which people can use to access services. However, if it is to work, the current direct payments system will require some adaptation. Currently, only people who are eligible for community care can receive direct payments, a relatively small group that does not directly correspond to people who need to access mental health services. In addition, modification of the provisions on direct payments will be required to enable their use in integrated social care and health settings. Finally, there would also need to be consideration of how people with fluctuating conditions access direct payments. It would be important to ensure easy transition, so that people did not feel that their recovery was being hampered through the loss of their personal budgets.

Greater choice brings many unanswered questions. In particular, there is an open question around how far people are responsible for the consequences of a poor choice, which has implications for the individual and the overall level of resources available for others. One way to guard against poor choices is to ensure that people are appropriately supported in making choices. The third working paper in this series set out what conditions would need to be in place to make choice a reality (Rankin 2005). These include increased resource capacity, better commissioning, use of individual care plans, a change in professional attitudes, creating roles for professionals and independent advocates to support choice and good information.

Ultimately, this 'trust me I'm a patient' approach heralds a step change in mental health policy. Choice holds out the prospect of more effective, more efficient services that are aligned to the interventions that work for each individual patient. Choice is also an end in itself, and could help to reinforce other agendas on rights and social inclusion.

(6) Refocusing of inpatient care
All mental health systems have to balance the needs of people who require crisis care with those of people who require long-term support, as well as with the needs of the general population. Although this report argues for greater focus on primary care, it remains vital to complete the reform of services for people who are acutely unwell. This could pay dividends in improving outcomes for service users and reducing stays on inpatient wards.

Research with service users and carers shows that people want some form of crisis support, but not necessarily in a hospital environment. Many people appealed for therapeutic places where people could be admitted for short periods to stabilise and manage a crisis (Rethink 2005).

Crisis units could help to redress the balance between patients and professionals by making greater use of advance directives. Advance directives allow people to make choices in anticipation of times when their capacity may be diminished. They are a formal (but not legally binding) record of the service user's wishes and NICE recommends their use where possible. The potential benefits include empowerment of the service user, better communication, tolerance for people with mental health problems, and a reduction in hospital services and judicial proceedings (Papageorgious et al 2004). In one randomised controlled trial, use of crisis plans did significantly reduce compulsory admissions under the Mental Health Act (Henderson et al 2004).

Elements of an alternative crisis unit

- Two stage admission process: admitted for observation and assessment and then decision made about future care

- Differentiates between the acute and recovery stages of the illness

- Person-centred care

- Short periods of care to avoid institutionalisation

- Offers a safe haven

- Therapeutic environment with natural open spaces and gardens

- One-to-one time with staff

- Private rooms

- Recreational activities

- 'Customer focus' – patients treated with respect

(Rethink 2005)

These six recommendations would help to create a community-orientated health system that offers a better response to people with mental health problems. However, mental health is an issue that is bigger than the health service and needs to be mainstreamed across other policy areas, including employment policy, education and social care. This requires co-ordinated leadership from both central and local government. As part B will discuss, lack of leadership has been one of the major barriers to change in mental health.

Part B Overcoming barriers to change

One thing policy-makers are never short of is prescriptions for change. Yet, taking a longer-term perspective, it is possible to see that policy ideas do get lost in practice. Often, there is a loss between the vision expressed by policy-makers and the day-to-day implementation of the policy. In the meantime priorities shift, new initiatives begin and champions move on. The gap between rhetoric and reality can be especially pronounced in relation to mental health (Mental Health Taskforce 2003).

This section considers the potential barriers to change and offers some thoughts as to how these can be overcome.

Resources

One of the most frequently cited barriers to any change is the level of resources. Traditionally seen as the 'Cinderella' service, some consider that mental health has been historically underfunded (Boardman 2005). As chapter 3 indicated, mental health services are generally of a lower standard than other parts of the health service. In order to deliver improvements in mental health, the Government needs to ensure an appropriate level of resources and their effective use.

Currently resources are not always used effectively. The continued reform of inpatient care, a reduction in the use of anti-depressants and a shift towards evidence-based talking therapies are all ways to make more effective use of scarce resources by ensuring that spending is linked to services that provide effective outcomes.

In the short term, moving to new kinds of services or treatments may require a transition fund. This would pay for the upfront costs of changing to new ways of working, for example training staff or funding new infrastructure.

Making better use of existing resources has to be an important element of an improved mental health service. Nevertheless, using resources more effectively does not necessarily mean that there will be any reductions in costs to the healthcare system. One study of effective treatments (including psychological treatments and drug treatments) showed that even when treatments were effective there was no apparent reduction in the demand for healthcare. This study suggested that there could be savings to the economy as a whole, but that costs in the healthcare sector are likely to rise (McCrone et al 2003). However, it has also been suggested that the return on expenditure on mental health can be high, compared with other health issues, because of the many negative external impacts that can be avoided (McDaid 2005).

At the time of writing, the current level of resources appears to be insufficient to deliver the necessary improvements. It has been argued that the true costs of implementing the National Service Framework (NSF) have not been allowed for, and that there will be a shortfall in the number of staff needed to meet its demands (Boardman 2005). As noted earlier, the Wanless Report stated that the additional annual cost of implementing the NSF would be £3.1 billion a year by 2010-11, roughly doubling spending (at 2002 levels) on mental health services for adults (Wanless 2002). Along with others (Layard 2005b), this paper calls for an expansion in the provision of talking therapies, which would probably require additional resources.

Spending on mental health is related to total spending on health. At the time of writing, it is unknown whether the Government will continue to increase spending on health as a proportion of GDP. However, after 2008, it seems possible that while the rate of growth on health spending might decline, spending as a proportion of GDP could still rise, as envisaged by the Wanless Report (Wanless 2002).

If this scenario is true, mental health is likely to share in the overall level of growth. Nevertheless, policy-makers need to ask whether this will be sufficient to deliver real improvements in mental health services. It is also necessary to consider the future level of demand. In developed countries mental health problems are set to grow as a proportion of total illnesses (WHO 2001). This is already evident in the UK: in 2005, for the first time more people were claiming Incapacity Benefit due to mental ill-health, than due to musculoskeletal problems (Henderson et al 2005).

As such, it appears that mental health will need an increased share of the health budget if we are to see improvements and an expansion of provision in primary care and health promotion. As a priority, the Government should review current spending on mental health in order to answer two questions:

- Is spending cost effective? (Is it linked into services that improve outcomes?)

- Is the level of spending on particular services sufficient?

Systems and structures

In the past, major structural changes to the NHS and social care system have been the first choice for governments that have been impatient for improvement. In the NHS, this shows no signs of abating with proposals for Payment by Results (PBR) and Practice Based Commissioning underway.[23] However, there is an inherent risk that designing and redesigning systems becomes a proxy for better outcomes. For this reason, further structural change seems unhelpful.

In relation to PBR, it is as yet unclear how it will work for mental health. The long-term and episodic nature of mental health problems and

---

23 Payment by Results (PBR) means that NHS Trusts will receive part of their income based on a fixed cost per case, rather than on a block contract basis. Although this only applies to parts of the acute sector, it will be extended to outpatient, community, mental health, and learning disability services. Practice Based Commissioning (PBC) means that primary care services will be assigned responsibilities for commissioning services. These systems may have a significant impact on many areas. Both PBR and PBC share the overarching aim of making services more responsive to patient preferences. For instance PBR means that money follows the patient, whilst PBC aims to improve commissioning by attuning it better to local needs.

diversity of services would make it difficult to classify cases for payment purposes.

Central government needs to ensure that the right incentives are in place for providers to supply good mental health care and for PCTs to prioritise mental health in their commissioning. As such this may require fine tuning, such as more focused targets to improve outcomes of people with mental health problems, such as targets on employment levels and access to healthcare.

Commissioning

The commissioning process is the starting point for good services. But across health and social care, there have been common concerns about the commissioning function. All too often it is partial and ineffective, with commissioners acting as purchasers, rather than taking on a strategic role that includes their other functions, such as needs assessment and monitoring services. It will also take time for PCTs to mature as commissioners (Roche 2004). There are particular difficulties in commissioning mental health services, which have been criticised for being neither needs-led nor locally-based (Light and Cohen 2003). In social care, local authorities are set to take on a more strategic commissioning role, which includes conducting a regular audit of local needs (Rankin and Regan 2004). This would be a helpful step for mental health, if done in collaboration with service users, local PCTs and commissioners of secondary care services.

User involvement

Service users should be routinely involved in setting priorities for service development. Of course, it is important not to underestimate the challenges in ensuring that user involvement is meaningful. As the experience of one trailblazing NHS trust has demonstrated, making user involvement a reality requires a major cultural shift (Perkins et al 2004). Service users have expressed common concerns that current involvement mechanisms can be meaningless and tokenistic. In focus groups, people described taking part in meetings that were promoted as consultation processes but were actually just communication vehicles for decisions that had already been taken (Rethink 2005).

However, it is undeniable that changes in attitudes and greater flexibility in running services have begun to occur through user involvement. The development of Patients' Councils and independent advocacy have given services users more influence over their care and treatment (Campbell 2005). Service user involvement needs to take place if services are to reflect local need and become better attuned to people's preferences. Service users have to be in positions of power to challenge the way services work.

Culture change

Culture change is easy to advocate, but difficult to achieve. Nevertheless, policy-makers need to continue to be concerned with changing cultures if recommendations are to make a difference on the ground. In the past, barriers to new ways of doing things in health and social care have come from a failure to follow institutional change with cultural change. There has been the assumption that a new structure automatically means 'culture change will just happen', or that 'we do this anyway', so there is no need to change (Peck et al 2001).

Culture change has particular relevance for mental health services where there is a history of discriminatory attitudes and poor practice (Keating et al 2002, Mental Health Taskforce 2003). The Government's programme on tackling stigma and discrimination shows that it recognises the importance of changing attitudes in health and social care services (NIMHE 2004). There is evidence to show the impact of educational interventions in the public sector, although what is missing is the strategy for implementing it (Mental Health Awareness in Action 2003). Significantly, the new Disability Discrimination Act places a positive duty on public sector employers to promote rights, rather than simply not discriminate.

Clearly, cultural change cannot be confined to services and there needs to be a cultural shift in social attitudes to mental health. Mental Health in the Mainstream is predicated on the idea that the mainstream undergoes a wider culture change. Bringing the mainstream to mental health means that people value mental health as a positive good and support the rights and inclusion of people with mental health problems. This is a very complex agenda, which encompasses many elements, including health promotion and anti-discrimination work (see SEU 2004, Friedli 2005). The role of the media is especially important. The media needs to enforce its own code of practice as set out by the Press Complaints Commission and National Union of Journalists. Both Government and the public can put greater pressure on these organisations to hold the media to account. The Stigma Stopwatch programme run in Scotland is one mechanism to ensure the media sticks to its own standards. Launched in 2003 by the See Me campaign, this is a web-based campaign that encourages members of the public to report good and bad practice in media discussions of mental health (see www.seemescotland.org/stigma/action.php).

Political ownership

One of the biggest barriers to delivering a different mental health policy has been the lack of political interest in and ownership of the issue. Within the Department of Health there is a Minister of State whose remit covers adult mental health services. But no matter how effective the individual is, they lack the high status to lead on the issue. Moreover their brief is restricted to 'services' rather than outcomes and the wider agenda on health promotion. The person who could make the difference is the Secretary of State for Health. However, as Anna Coote has pointed out, holders of this post are more accurately described as the Secretary of State for the NHS (Coote 2003). In recent years, the Secretary of State for Health has not been prominent in discussions about the future of mental health, and policies for mental health promotion share the wider problems that afflict the whole public health agenda. Public health doesn't fit into the electoral cycle. Interventions to secure better public health or reduce heath inequalities take a generation to show their effects, whilst a new target on hospital waiting lists can be achieved over the course of a Parliament.

This report has proposed a greater role for community-based primary care. But the demise of past initiatives, such as Health Action Zones, offers some lessons on the potential pitfalls facing local initiatives without long-term buy-in from central government. Health Action Zones were abandoned in 2002, just as they were becoming established. This is indicative of central government's wavering commitment to public health and decentralisation. If there is to be a shift to community-based mental health (as this report proposes), there also needs to be a change in approach from central government.

Central government needs to allow local services to develop on the basis of an inclusive commissioning process that takes into account local needs. However, the role for central government is no less important. If mental health is to be transformed, there need to be high-profile champions within government. The evolution of policy around childcare shows how this might work. A decade ago, no front-line politician made major speeches or policy announcements on childcare. But the cause of children – their life chances, early years and care – was championed by a small group in central government and other policy-makers. It has now moved to the political centre stage and few would dispute the economic and social importance of having a policy on childcare.

There are several measures that could help to focus greater attention on mental health. The Department of Health could be reorientated by creating a Secretary of State for Health and Wellbeing and an Under-Secretary of State for the NHS (Coote 2003). Theoretically, this could focus political attention on complete physical and mental health. It could be a platform to ensure that mental health is in the mainstream of other developments in health policy, something which has not always been true. In addition, the Office of Disability Issues will also provide some strategic leadership in ensuring the delivery of rights for people with long-term disabilities (SEU 2005).

But, as has been discussed, mental health problems touch on many areas of life and the issue of mental health is relevant many parts of the public sector. This calls for some kind of co-ordinating role, an individual who can champion the cause of mental health across the public sector, whilst being independent from government. To this end, this report proposes considering developing a role for a National Commissioner for Mental Health. The purpose of this role would not be to duplicate the position of the National Director for Mental Health (known as the 'mental health tsar') based in the health service. Rather, their function would be analogous to the role of the National Children's Commissioner. The National Commissioner for Mental Health would be an independent voice to champion mental health issues across different government departments. They would also encourage stakeholders to explore the mental health implications of different areas of public policy to assess the impact on mental health.

The question of political ownership is critical. At the time of writing, there has never been so much attention devoted to mental health from government. But, strangely, it remains a non-issue in many political debates. The Government has ambitions on mental health promotion, reducing health inequalities and better services (DH 1999), as well as other relevant policies focused on improving the rights of disabled people and access to the labour market (Strategy Unit 2005). If these goals are to be met and mental health is to move into the mainstream of policy it will only do so with strong political ownership.

Conclusion

Do we have a mentally healthy future? This report looks ahead to 2025 and envisages a society that thinks about mental health in a very different way: where mental health is valued and promoted, and people with mental health problems have the right kind of treatment and support to meet their health and social needs.

There are compelling reasons to act to move towards this vision. Mental health problems have a high human cost in terms of lost opportunities, poorer health and lower life expectancy. They disproportionately affect disadvantaged groups and are bound up with poverty and social exclusion. But also, mental health problems carry substantial economic costs.

In the last twenty years, there have been some important changes in mental health services, and the years since 1997 have resulted in some more attention to mental health. But there needs to be a further shift towards protecting and promoting the mental health of the whole community. Among policy-makers, there are reasonable levels of knowledge and understanding of how to treat mental health problems and promote mental health, but this is not always reflected in the reality of people's day-to-day experiences in health services. Some of the elements necessary for improvements in mental health are in place, although not always as part of a complete strategy for mental health.

Mental health should be a major concern for policy-makers. Rebalancing the mental health system towards community-based primary care holds out the promise of a better response to mental health problems, where mental health is valued. But if this is to become a reality by 2025, there needs to be sustained political leadership. These issues are too important to be ignored.

Appendix: Rethink qualitative research with service users and carers

In spring 2005, Rethink conducted qualitative research with service users and carers who were in touch with Rethink services. The research explored the kind of services that people would like to see in the future.

There were three groups of carers and three groups of service users.

Breakdown of service users' data

Gender	Male = 6 (46.2%) Female = 7 (53.8%)
Age	Average age = 41.4 years Minimum age = 27 years Maximum age = 60 years
Ethnic origin	White British = 10 (76.9%) British Asian/Asian = 324 (23.1%)
Time as a service user	Average = 9.2 years Minimum = 3 years Maximum = 20 years Not known = 3
Diagnosis	Psychosis = 1 (7.7%) Schizophrenia = 1 (7.7%) Paranoid schizophrenia = 1 (7.7%) Depression with self harm = 1 (7.7%) Anxiety and depression = 2 (15.4%) Other inc. 'Mental breakdown' = 4 (30.8%) Not known = 3 (23.0%)
Total	**13**

Breakdown of carers' data

Gender	Male = 4 (20%) Female = 16 (80%)
Age	Average age= 59.6 years Minimum age = 47 years Maximum age = 75 years

---

24 Data incomplete

Ethnic origin	White British = 16 (80%)
	White European = 1 (5%)
	British Asian/Asian25 = 3 (15%)
Time as a carer	Average = 8.3 years
	Minimum = 1.5 years
	Maximum = 20 years
	Not known = 5
Relationship to the person they are caring for	Son/daughter = 12 (60%)
	Mother/father = 1 (5%)
	Partner = 3 (15%)
	No relation = 1 (5%)
	Not known = 3 (15%)
Diagnosis of the person they are caring for	Dual diagnosis = 4 (20%)
	Psychosis = 3 (15%)
	Schizophrenia = 6 (30.0%)
	Schizo-typical personality disorder = 1 (5.0%)
	Paranoid schizophrenia = 1 (5.0%)
	Depression with self harm = 1 (5.0%)
	Bi-polar disorder = 1 (5.0%)
	Not known = 3 (15.0%)
Total	**20**

References

Acheson D (1998) *Independent inquiry into inequalities in health*, HMSO

Akroyd S, Wyllie A (2002) *Impacts of a national media campaign to counter stigma and discrimination associated with mental illness:* Research Report for Ministry of Health, New Zealand

Arksey H (2002) 'Scoping the field: services for carers of people with mental health problems', *Health and social care in the community* 11 (4)

Association of the British Pharmaceutical Industry (ABPI)/Long Term Medical Conditions Alliance (LMCA) (2002) *Quality of life, its role in health care decisions*

Astbury J (1999) *Gender and mental health*: Global Health Equity Initiative Project at the Harvard Center for Population and Development Studies

Barnes M et al (1999) *Unequal partners: user groups and community care* Policy Press

Bhugra D (2000) 'Migration and schizophrenia', *Acta Psychiatrica Scandanavia* 102

BIHR (2002) *Something for everyone* British Institute of Human Rights

Boardman J (2005) 'New services for old', chapter 2 from *Beyond the water towers* The Sainsbury Centre for Mental Health

Boardman J (2003) 'Work, employment and psychiatric disability, *Advances in Psychiatric Treatment* 9

Boardman J et al (2004) 'Needs for mental health treatment among GP attendees', *British Journal of Psychiatry* 185

Bond G et al (2001) 'Implementing supported employment as an evidence-based practice', *Psychiatric Services* 52 (3)

Borg M and Kristiansen K (2004) 'Recovery-orientated professionals: helping relationships in mental health services', *Journal of Mental Health* 13 (5)

Braunholtz S et al (2004) '*Well? What do you think? The second national Scottish survey of public attitudes to mental health, mental well-being and mental health problems* Research Findings No. 44, Health and Community Care Research Programme

Burns T (2004) *Community mental health teams* OUP

Butler F (2004) *Human rights: who needs them?* ippr

CAB (2004) *Out of the picture – CAB evidence on mental health and social exclusion* Citizens Advice Bureau

Campbell P (2005) 'From little acorns, the mental health service user movement', chapter 6 from *Beyond the water towers* The Sainsbury Centre for Mental Health

Catty J et al (2001) 'Day centres for severe mental illness' *Cochrane Database Systematic Review* 2001 (2): CD001710

Clark C, ed (2001) *Adult day services and social inclusion* Jessica Kingsley

Collishaw et al (2004) 'Time trends in adolescent mental health', *Journal of Child Psychology and Psychiatry* 45

CHI (2003) *What CHI has found in mental health trusts* Commission for Health Improvement

Coote A (2003) 'A fourth way for health policy', *Renewal* 11 (3)

Coote A et al (2004) *Finding out what works – understanding complex, community based initiatives* The King's Fund

Craig T et al (2004) 'The Lambeth Early Onset (LEO) Team: randomised controlled trial of the effectiveness of specialised care for early psychosis', *British Medical Journal* 329

Crisp A (2003) 'An update on the college's anti-stigma campaign website' *Psychiatric Bulletin* 27

Crisp A et al (2000) 'Stigmatisation of people with mental illnesses', *The British Journal of Psychiatry* 177

Crowther R et al (2001) 'Helping people with severe mental illness to obtain work: a systematic review' *British Medical Journal* 322

Dean H (2002) *Welfare rights and social policy* Pearson Education

DH (2005a) *Delivering Choosing Health* Department of Health

DH (2005b) *Delivering race equality in mental health care* Department of Health

DH (2005c) *Independence, well-being and choice* The Stationery Office

DH (2004a) *National Service Framework for children, young people and maternity services* Department of Health and Department for Education and Skills

DH (2004b) *Choosing Health* Department of Health

DH (2004c) *The National Service Framework for mental health – five years on* Department of Health

DH (2004d) *'Choose and book' – patients' choice of hospital and booked appointment* Department of Health

DH (2004e) *Organising and delivering psychological therapies* Department of Health

DH (2003) *Building on the best, choice, responsiveness and equity in the NHS* Department of Health

DH (2002) *Developing services for carers and families of people with mental illness* Department of Health

DH (2000) *The NHS Plan, a plan for investment, a plan for reform* Department of Health

DH (1999) *National Service Framework for mental health* Department of Health

DTI (2005) *Work and families, choice and flexibility, a consultation document* Department of Trade and Industry

Diffley C (2003) *Managing mental health* The Work Foundation

DRC (2004) *Equal treatment – closing the gap* Disability Rights Commission

DRC (2003) *Coming together – mental health service users and disability rights*, Disability Rights Commission (available from www.drc-gb.org)

DWP (2005) *Five year strategy, opportunity and security throughout life* Department for Work and Pensions

DWP (2004) *Incapacity Benefit – quarterly report* Department for Work and Pensions

Evandrou M and Glaser K (2003) 'Combining work and family life: the pension penalty of caring', *Ageing and Society* 23

Faulkner A (2000) *Strategies for living: a report of user led research into people's strategies for living with mental distress* Mental Health Foundation

Forrest E (2005) 'Must try harder', *Health Service Journal Supplement* 31 March

Forrest E (2004) 'The right to choose', *Health Service Journal* 9 December

Friedli L (2005) *Choosing mental health – a policy agenda for mental health and public health* The Mental Health Foundation

Gillen (2005) '10,000 miles to go in improving mental health services', *Community Care* 17 March

Glendinning R et al (2002) *Well? What do you think? A national Scottish survey of public attitudes to mental health, well being and mental health problems* Research Findings 27, Scottish Executive

Greatly A and Ford R (2002) *Out of the maze – reaching and supporting Londoners with Severe Mental Health Problems* The Kings Fund/The Sainsbury Centre for Mental Health.

Hartley Brewer E (2001) *Learning to trust and trusting to learn* ippr

Healthcare Commission (2004a) *Healthcare Commission patient survey* Commission for Healthcare Audit and Inspection

Healthcare Commission (2004b) *NHS Performance Ratings 2003/2004* Commission for Healthcare Audit and Inspection

Heer B and Woodhead D (2002) *Promoting health, preventing illness* The King's Fund

Henderson C et al (2004) 'Effect of joint crisis plans on use of compulsory treatment in psychiatry: single blind randomised controlled trial', *British Medical Journal* 329

Henderson M et al (2005) 'Long term sickness', *British Medical Journal* 330

HM Treasury (2004) *2004 Spending Review, new public spending plans 2005-2008*

House of Commons Health Committee (2005) *The influence of the pharmaceutical industry: 4th report of the session 2004-05*, The Stationery Office

House of Commons/House of Lords: Joint Committee on Human Rights, Minutes of Evidence (available at www.publications.parliament.uk)

Howard League for Penal Reform (2003) *Busy doing nothing: the experience of 18-20 year old men on remand* (available at www.howardleague.org/publications)

Howard M (2004) *Equal citizenship and incapacity benefit reform:* paper to ippr seminar on the future of Incapacity Benefits, Disability Rights Commission

Huxley J and Thornicroft G (2003) Social inclusion, social quality and mental illness *British Journal of Psychiatry* 182

Joint Committee (2005) *Joint Committee on the Draft Mental Health Bill (reports I-III)* (available at www.publications.parliament.uk

Keating et al (2002) *Breaking the circles of fear* London: The Sainsbury Centre for Mental Health

Kim-Cohen J et al (2003) 'Prior juvenile diagnoses in adults with mental disorder - developmental follow back of a prospective-longitudinal cohort' *Archives of General Psychiatry* July, PubMed

Knapp M (2003) 'Hidden costs of mental illness' *British Journal of Psychiatry* 182

Knapp M et al (2004) *Mental health policy and practice across Europe, proposal for analytical study* European Observatory on Health Systems and Policies (available at www.euro.who.int/observatory)

Langan J and Lindow V (2004) *Mental health service users and their involvement in risk assessment and management* Joseph Rowntree Foundation

Layard R (2005a) *Happiness: lessons from a new science* Penguin

Layard R (2005b) *Mental health: Britain's biggest social problem?* (available at www.strategy.gov.uk)

Laurance J (2003) *Pure madness: how fear drives the mental health system* Routledge

Le Grand J (2003) *Individual choice and social exclusion:* CASE paper 75, Centre for Analysis of Social Exclusion at London School of Economics

Lehman A et al (2004) *Evidence-based mental health treatments and services* Millbank Memorial Fund

Light D and Cohen A (2003) *Commissioning Mental Health Services* The Sainsbury Centre for Mental Health

The Living Project Steering Group (2004) *The Living Project: research progress report* College Research Unit, Royal College of Psychiatrists and The First Step Trust (available at www.rcpsych.ac.uk)

Longley M et al (2001) *Promoting mental health in a civil society: towards a strategic approach* London: Nuffield Trust Publications

McCrone P et al (2003) *Mental Health Service Activity in London* The King's Fund

McCulloch A et al (2003) 'The NSF for mental health: past, present and future' *Mental Health Review* 8 (4)

McDaid D (2005a) *Mental health 1 – key issues in the development of policy and practice across Europe* European Observatory on Health Systems and Policies

McDaid D and Thornicroft G (2005b) *Mental health 2 – balancing institutional and community based care* European Observatory on Health Systems and Policies

McDaid D et al (2005c) *Mental health 3 – funding mental health in Europe* European Observatory on Health Systems and Policies

Meltzer et al (2000) *Mental health of children and adolescents in Great Britain* The Stationery Office

Mental Health Awareness in Action (2003) *How Can We Make Mental Health Education Work* (available at www.rethink.org)

The Mental Health Foundation (2005) *Up and running? Exercise therapy and the treatment of mild or moderate depression in primary care* The Mental Health Foundation

The Mental Health Foundation (2005) *Pull yourself together! A survey of stigma and discrimination faced by people who experience mental distress* The Mental Health Foundation

Mental Health Taskforce (2003) *Mental health taskforce report, choice responsiveness and equity* Department of Health

Mentality (2002) *Mental health improvement: what works? A briefing for the Scottish Executive* Scottish Executive and Mentality

Mind (2004a) *Ward watch* Mind (available at www.mind.org.uk)

Mind (2004b) *Not alone? Isolation and mental distress* Mind (available at www.mind.org.uk)

Mind (2002) *Mind's policy on primary care* Mind (available at www.mind.ac.uk)

MORI (2003) *Britain's attitudes to cancer* MORI (available at www.mori.com/polls)

National Statistics (2003) *Attitudes to mental illness 2003 report* Department of Health

NICE (2004) *Depression: management of depression in primary and secondary care* National Collaborating Centre for Mental Health and National Institute for Clinical Excellence

NICE (2002) *Full guidance on the use of newer (atypical) antipsychotic drugs for the treatment of schizophrenia* National Institute for Health and Clinical Excellence

NIMHE (2004) *From here to equality. A strategic plan to tackle discrimination on mental health grounds* National Institute for Mental Health in England and Department of Health

NIMHE (2002) *Cases for change, primary care* National Institute for Mental Health in England

Neuberger J (2005) *The moral state we're in* Harper Collins

Norwich Union Healthcare (2004) *Guide to services for a healthy mind* Norwich Union Health Care and Dr Foster

O'Connor W and Nazroo J (2002) *Ethnic differences in the context and experience of psychiatric illnesses, a qualitative study* On behalf of the Department of Health by the National Centre for Social Research and the Department of Epidemiology and Public Health at the Royal Free and University College Medical School

Ogilvie S (2003) *Barriers to employment, training and education for carers of people with severe mental illness* Rethink

ONS (2002) *Carers in Britain* Office of National Statistics

Papageorgious A et al (2004) 'Advance directives for patients compulsorily admitted to hospital with serious mental disorders' *Journal of Mental Health* 2004 (13)

Paxton (2004) 'Better organisation for psychological therapies in the NHS' *British Journal of Healthcare Management* February 2004

Peck E et al (2001) 'The meanings of 'Culture' in health and social care: a case study of the Combined Trust in Somerset' *Journal of Interprofessional Care*, 15 (4)

Perkins R et al (2004) 'Reality out of the rhetoric: user involvement in a mental health trust' *Mental Health Review* 9 (1)

Pelosi A and Birchwood M (2002) 'Is Early Intervention for psychosis a waste of valuable resources', *British Journal of Psychiatry* 182 196-8

Priebe S and Slade M (ed.) (2003) *Evidence in mental health care* Brunner-Routledge

Rankin J (2005a) *A good choice for mental health, working paper 3* ippr (available at www.ippr.org)

Rankin J (2005b) *Mental health and social inclusion, working paper 2* ippr (available at www.ippr.org)

Rankin J (2004) *Developments and trends in mental health policy, working paper 1* ippr (available at www.ippr.org)

Rankin J and Regan S (2004) *Meeting complex needs: the future of social care* ippr

Rethink (2005) *A summary of service user and carer focus group discussion:* unpublished manuscript, Rethink.

Rethink (2004) *Lost and found: voices from the forgotten generation* Rethink

Rethink (2003a) *Just 1%* Rethink

Rethink (2003b) *Who cares?* Rethink

Roche D (2004) *PCTs – an unfinished agenda?* ippr

Ryan (2002) 'Mental health' *Research Matters* 13, 2002

Sainsbury Centre (2003) *Fair for all, personal to you, consultation on choice, responsiveness and equity* The Sainsbury Centre for Mental Health

Sainsbury Centre (2002) *An executive briefing on primary care mental health services* The Sainsbury Centre for Mental Health

Salvage J (2002) *Rethinking professionalism, the first step for patient focused care* ippr (available at www.ippr.org)

Sayce L (2004) 'Risk, rights and anti-discrimination work in mental health: avoiding the risks in considering risk.' Adams R, Dominelli L and Payne M (eds) *Social Work Futures* Palgrave Macmillan

Sayce L and Boardman J (2003) 'The Disability Discrimination Act 1995: implications for psychiatrists' *Advances in Psychiatric Treatment* 9

Sayce L (2000) *From psychiatric patient to citizen* Macmillan

Scottish Executive (2004) *National programme for improving health and well-being – annual review 2003-04* Scottish Executive

Secker J (2000) *Accommodations and support required for the success of open employment for mental health service users* (available at www.regard.ac.uk)

Seddon D et al (2004) 'Supporting carers in paid employment' *Quality in Ageing* 5(1) June

Shimitras L et al (2003) 'Time use of people living with schizophrenia in north London catchment areas' *British Journal of Occupational Therapy* February

Sigle Ruston W (2004) *Intergenerational and life course transmission of social exclusion in the 1970 British Cohort Study* CASE Paper 78, Centre for Analysis for Social Exclusions LSE

Singleton N et al (2000) *Psychiatric morbidity among adults living in private households* Office for National Statistics, The Stationery Office

Singleton N et al (1998) *Psychiatric morbidity among prisoners, a summary report* Office for National Statistics, The Stationery Office

Smith M (2002) 'Stigma', *Advances in Psychiatric Treatment* (8)

SEU (2005) *Excluded older people* Social Exclusion Unit, Office of the Deputy Prime Minister

SEU (2004) *Mental health and social exclusion* Social Exclusion Unit, Office of the Deputy Prime Minister

SPRU (2004) *Hearts and minds, the health effects of caring*: Social Policy Research Unit, The University of York and Carers UK

Stanley K and Maxwell D (2004) *Fit for purpose?* ippr

Stanley K and Regan S (2003) *The missing million* ippr

Stanley L, Lohde L and White S (2004) *Sanctions and sweeteners* ippr

Strategy Unit (2005) *Improving the life chances of disabled people:* A joint report with DWP, DH, DfES and ODPM

Thornicroft G, Tansella M (1999) *The mental health matrix* Cambridge University Press

TSO *Mental health (care and treatment) (Scotland) Act 2003* The Stationery Office

Wallcraft J (2003) *Choice, responsiveness and equity in mental health: report from Jan Wallcraft to the Mental Health Task Group on views of hard-to-reach service users* Unpublished manuscript

Wanless D (2002) *Securing our future health: taking a long-term view. Final report* HM Treasury

Wanless D (2001) *Securing our future health: taking a long-term view. Interim report* HM Treasury

Warner L (2005) 'Acute care in crisis', chapter 3 from *Beyond the water towers:* The Sainsbury Centre for Mental Health

White M and Angus J (2003) *Arts and mental health literature review* Centre for Arts and Humanities in Health and Medicine

WHO (2004a) *Prevention of mental disorders* World Health Organisation

WHO (2004b) *Promoting mental health* World Health Organisation

WHO (2003) *Investing in mental health* World Health Organisation

WHO (2001) *Mental health – new understanding, new hope* World Health Organisation